Price 37½ Cents.

NEW YORK:
W. F. BURGESS.
1850.

NEW YORK IN SLICES:

BY

AN EXPERIENCED CARVER:

BEING

THE ORIGINAL SLICES PUBLISHED IN THE N. Y. TRIBUNE.

REVISED, ENLARGED, AND CORRECTED

BY THE AUTHOR.

WITH SPLENDID ILLUSTRATIONS.

NEW YORK:
W. F. BURGESS 22, ANN STREET.
1849.

INTRODUCTION.

A GREAT city is the highest result of human civilization. Here the Soul, that most perfect and godlike of all created things, the essence and spirit of the visible world, has put forth all its most wonderful energies—energies developed to their utmost power, and excited to their highest state of activity by constant contact with countless other souls, each emulating, impelling, stimulating, rivalling, outdoing the others. What a world of thought and wisdom and imagination and benevolence and friendship and love ought we not to expect from this mighty concentration of so many immortalities, so many heavenly faculties! The very atmosphere should be purified and brightened by the incessant flashing of the electricity of intellect, and a boundless horizon of sympathies and affections, rising from all these noble hearts, should spread above the dwelling-place of so many glorious spirits, reminding them always of their heavenly origin, and keeping ever in view their lofty destiny on earth—to sanctify this material life and this all-beautiful world to God and to each other. Yes—man in isolation, or thinly gathered in feeble neighborhoods and scattered villages, is powerless to accomplish great works, or to fulfil the mission of his race. It is only in a large city, where some hundreds of thousands combine their various powers, that the human mind can efficiently stamp itself on every thing by which it is surrounded—can transmute the insensible earth to a fit temple and dwelling-place for immortal spirits. What do we see?

Reluctantly we turn our gaze from the broad Bay, in whose musical undulations sleeps the sweet spirit of Peace and Beauty, fanned by the sphere-wandering winds. The silken rustle of the leaves overhead, hushing the pale-blue chameleon in his noontide dream of air, sheds a slumberous shower upon us. But we are not here for slumber. Let us on through this broad gravelled walk, arched by shady old trees, and hasten to emerge into the street, where our dream will be soon enough broken by the ceaseless noises that roll in sea-like waves down from the clamorous city. What a grand avenue, mounting the subdued hill that like a gigantic camel patiently stoops to bear its huge burden! Look, how beautiful the prospect! The eye, sinking beneath this pressure of imposing forms, loses itself in the far-reaching sweep of the street, terminated by a confused cloud of moving wheels, fronts of houses, and thickened air, pierced here and there with a tall spire or swelling dome. Here at our very feet springs up into the air a lofty steeple, stately as a palm and graceful as an exhalation. Within this Gothic porch—but of that anon. Look away to the right, down this immense granite artery, whence pours the turbid flood of trade and money, gain and traffic. Hark! a dull, sullen growl comes up from its lowest depths, as of the groans of the victims hourly choked and thrust down beneath the wave, mingled with the low chuckle and the hollow laugh of the victors—themselves, it may be, doomed to be vanquished in the next moment, and sent to join their victims on "the night's Plutonian shore," where limp the ghosts of lame ducks which no man can number.

But all this is underground, or hidden behind the massive gray columns. To our eye nothing appears but a panorama of palaces, variegated with eager groups of men apparently engaged in the discussion of lofty themes, upon which hang most momentous issues. And so they do—the "settlement" of weekly balances and the "issues" of country banks. 'Tis a magnificent avenue of architectural beauty—the Acropolis of this modern Athens—only all these splendid temples are erected to one divinity, all these crowds of devotees worship the same god,—MAMMON.

But let us watch an opening between the thronging procession of spacious and gayly painted carriages, whose accommodating drivers beckon you at every corner to a ride upon their crimson cushions, and darting adroitly through, as none but a well-practised citizen can do, regain the fashionable side of Broadway—for you must remember that nothing could more effectually stamp you as vulgar than to be seen stumbling over the crockery-crates and second-hand furniture of the shilling pavement. Let us hurry by this other dusty old graveyard—for the dead have nothing to say for us—and past this palatial refectory cooled by a julep-fountain in the basement and a *jet de Croton* in the court, and so pursue our walk. Here on the right, stooping gracefully in her dazzling bath, and drawing her scarf of rainbows coquettishly about her shoulders, stands the fair Maid of the Mist, cooling the air with her dewy breath; and yonder, embowered amid these shady vistas, another palace rears its marble front. Glorious City! happy people! nothing but palaces and carriages and hostelries—fountains and shady walks, splendor, refinement, luxury, and ease! And see here—whole miles of plate-glass, interspersed with the most exquisite, rare, and costly fabrics, amid which and courteously waited upon by handsome and happy men, sit enthroned in silk beautiful ladies, selecting with the deliberation worthy so momentous a subject, the robes in which to enshrine their lovely forms. One can almost imagine he sees the houris selecting each a rosy cloud to waft her to the happy soul to whom she is to minister. Can these splendid creatures know trouble or sorrow—and are not their homes the abode of peace and love and every joy? We cannot penetrate the sacred mysteries of the fireside; but could we read the secret history of fashionable life and fashionable folly, we should encounter such a record of broken hearts, broken faith, broken vows, and violated honor, as would make the soul recoil in horror and amazement to find that all this brilliant and dazzling display of wealth and beauty and taste and refinement was but the fantastic and mocking mask of a wide-yawning domestic hell. Yes—not the beggar's den nor the murderer's cell could vomit forth ghastlier agonies than stalk through the magnificent saloons, and hide behind the silken curtains where gather Fashion's sparkling throng.

But let us leave this false magnificence, with all its dire realities made more horrible by the contrast, and go among the naked and apparent miseries of the metropolis. There are four hundred thousand people here who live somehow—and we have seen but a small portion of them in our walk thus far. Let us turn a little to the right—or left, for it is the same for our purpose—and now stop your nose! for the horrible stench of the poverty, misery, beggary, starvation, crime, filth, and licentiousness that congregate in our Large City, of which we were just now so boastful, as being the highest work of human mind and genius, comes reeking round the corner, and in a moment we shall stand by the very rotting skeleton of City Civilization. In these low, squalid huts, piled one upon another, without space for a man to breathe or a sunbeam to flash between—in these dank, floorless cellars, whose blight and mildew ooze from the very walls, and the air is as cold and dead as in a charnel-house—are crowded two hundred and fifty thousand men, women, and children within a space not fitly capable for more than one-tenth their number. And these are the very people, too, who do nearly all the real work of the whole City, whose brows sweat, and whose muscles ache with the toil which all ought to share, and who, it would seem, should be lodged and cared for in honor as public benefactors. But so does not Civilization order it. Here are thirty thousand women and young girls, who work ten, twelve, fourteen hours a day for that which scarcely, with the strictest economy, procures them the merest necessary food and cheapest rags to cover them. In summer they have work and hunger—while in winter they have sometimes only hunger and cold, for work is often scarce in winter, and the competition for the liberty of working sixteen hours for a shilling is so great! Now then you are ready to hear, too, that in these quarters abide ten thousand public prostitutes—their blood inflamed with cheap and poisoned alcohol, their bodies slowly rotting with the foulest and most loathsome disease, their tongues incessantly uttering blasphemy and obscenity. Is woman, then, so much more depraved than man? By no means. There are in this very City fifty thousand men morally as guilty as these ten thousand women. But Civilization does not punish the men. It is only the sufferers who are guilty. Toiling from infancy in starvation and filthy rags, working the very life out of them through many a weary week and month and year, they could not help but see, as they looked through the dark windows of their gloomy cells, the daughters of infamy flaunting along in idle and fantastic splendor. Is it strange that so many ask themselves the question, Why shall I be thus a martyr to that virtue that will not even bring me bread? Nay, is it not wonderful that so many yet withstand the temptation? and ought not Society to accuse itself for thus driving Woman to want and starvation, and then encouraging with a promise of impunity the libertine to lay his devilish nets in which to ensnare her soul and body?

In this gay and beautiful City, too, so full of palaces and pleasures, there are seventy thousand confessed paupers, most of whom are maintained, some in sickness, and all in despair, at other "palaces" which the city has built around its suburbs. In the centre of the town is also another huge "palace" full of malefactors and magistrates, policemen, and petty larceny rogues, drunkards, vagrants, rioters, negroes, and wretches of every grade and aspect of misery; and on a beautiful green island surrounded by peaceful and transparent waters—for they have not yet reached the turbulent City—are other "palaces" also built and maintained at great cost to the good citizens, and whose noisome and infected cells, not bigger nor higher than coffins, are crammed with wretches, layer above layer, and oh, so horribly filthy, worm-eaten, and abominable, that Death would blush through his grinning skeleton to call them his! Five hundred of such poor wretches are sometimes crowded into a single room where there is not absolutely space enough for them all to lie down at once and die! In other portions of the establishment you meet with gangs of blear-eyed drunkards with their poor brains vacillating fearfully between idiocy and madness—here are groups of diseased and abandoned women pouring out blasphemies and all the atrocities of language in a manner that would make the most hardened man-villain shudder, (for angels when they fall are your only true fiends!)—and yonder a chain-gang of human cattle driven to their toil with lash and oath. This is denominated by our wise and benevolent rulers the *penitentiary* institution—chiefly, one would imagine, that such a thing as penitence there were utterly and forever impossible. Why, Purity itself in such contact must soon become foul as Acheron. But all this is unheard of by the City Fathers in the "Tea-Room;" and if occasionally the Corporation have a Champagne frolic at Blackwell's Island, or an extempore cold snack at Long-Island Farms, the papers of their party go into ecstasies at "the prompt and vigorous performance of their public duties by our present Corporation, so unlike their corrupt predecessors"—and there an end!

So dwindle away the glories of our magnificent City, which, stripped of the cloud of appearances in which it is veiled, looks but a vast abyss of crime and suffering, with here and there a crystal shooting out over the horrid recess of filth. These are but a few of the black shadows which the City throws across our glass; but they may serve as an outline sketch of a picture we shall proceed to fill up in detail. Is this, then, the highest result of human intellect? Is it not infinitely inferior to a Beaver-Dam?

Museum. BROADWAY. Astor-House.

NEW YORK IN SLICES.

Slice I.—BROADWAY.

Broadway narrowly escapes being the most magnificent street in the world. If the money expended upon it, architecturally, had been guided by half a grain of true taste or even common sense, the effect would have been perfectly glorious. As it is, we have the chaotic elements of a noble avenue, the contemplation of which gives us more pain than pleasure. We admire variety, as well as another; and especially in city architecture should monotony and tameness be avoided. But the laws of diversity are as strict and as imperative as the requirements of good morals or a good dinner; and the moment the eye is offended with unmeaning incongruity or unsymmetrical abruptness, that instant we have left the realm of taste, and crossed the boundary of chaos. In music there are nearly as many discords as concords; but the proper distribution of the discords, according to the immutable laws of proportion, is all that distinguishes harmony from the tuning of the instruments. Take any block in Broadway, and imagine the cost of its construction judiciously laid out under the supervision of a true artist, and you will at once conceive the present mean and insignificant superfice of expensive materials expanded into a spacious and continuous front, palatial in its aspect, and ennobling in its design. Carry out this process from the Bowling Green to Grace Church, and you will see an avenue of palaces and temples two miles and a half in length, and displaying every variety of architectural beauty—now the pure and intellectual Grecian, in its various exquisite forms; now the massive Gothic, the picturesque Roman, or the solemn Egyptian—each square outvying its neighbor, and every step conducting you to new beauties. Such would be the result of an association of capital and intelligence, of a far-seeing and comprehensive knowledge of the true end and aim of material forms and their influence upon character and public taste and morals. You may smile at our attribution of a moral agency to granite, bricks, and marble; and yet such is our religion. The constant and unobtrusive presence of forms of real beauty, whether in music, painting, sculpture, or architecture, or in the "daily beauty" of good deeds and expansive affections, exerts a chastening and elevating influence upon all mankind. Who shall deny this ministration of the beautiful, or set a limit to its beneficent effects?

To the man of taste, Broadway as it is appears like an interminable collection of richly-stored bazaars, hastily erected to meet the emergencies of trade and traffic, and only intended for temporary use. Many of them, it is true, are gorgeous with plate-glass and gilded embellishments, squandered with prodigality, but without taste, and catching the eye for an instant by the glare of a false and frivolous ambition. A few really fine structures also, here and there, meet the eye; but they appear like exhalations from an incredible extent of rubbish. A long, low row of unmeaning outlines and angles that geometry would blush to own. Here a brick schoolhouse, there a clapboard barn; now a penitentiary, and then a pound; now stumbling over a rotten cellar-door, and anon walking through an obtrusive plate-glass window, stuffed with gaudy cashmeres and mildewed muslins. This is the external appearance of Broadway. While, if you venture to raise your eyes above the level of your nose, an interminable line of crooked well-posts, armed with glass bottles, and held together by wire clotheslines, meets your gaze. You search in vain for even some faint acknowledgment of the line of proportion and continuation, and involuntarily wish for darkness to conceal the jagged and unfinished upper story of magnificent Broadway. How easy it would have been to have had the entire street lined with elegant edifices, rising and falling by harmonious degrees, and studded with classic porticoes and rich balconies!

But notwithstanding these glaring defects of taste, Broadway is, as times go, a very noble street; altogether the most showy, the most crowded, and the richest fashionable thoroughfare on the continent, and surpassed by not more than three or four in Europe. Washington-street of Boston, Chesnut-street of Philadelphia, and Chartres-street of New Orleans, although each attractive in its way, would not altogether make a fair match for Broadway, either in costliness or appearance; and as for business, you could pour all three of them into Broadway, at any hour of the day, without perceptibly swelling its current. Taking it altogether, notwithstanding its want of architectural harmony, Broadway well deserves its reputation as the centre of fashion and republican aristocracy. The shops are more numerous, more extensive, and filled with more expensive and rarer assortments of goods than those of any other street in America; and this superiority is so unquestionable, that all other cities involuntarily accept the *cue* from the dealers in Broadway. In fact, for the world of fashionable shopperesses, who expend money purely from extravagance, to be out of Broadway is to be in a vulgar and barbarous state of existence.

The great commercial feature of Broadway is its immense and unrivalled fancy drygoods establishments. Besides the palace of my Lord Stewart, with its exquisite marble front and mean brick ends, there are at least a dozen drygoods establishments in Broadway, each of which requires a princely income for its support. These immense stores are always full, at shopping hours, with the sauntering Queens, Duchesses, and Countesses of Republican New York, half buried amid heaps of exquisite and costly fabrics, and endeavoring by the help of finery which they do not want, to stimulate their jaded and satiated tastes and ambitions, or to wile away the dreary hours between one scene and another of fashionable dissipation. Notwithstanding the gorgeousness of their employment, it is sad enough to look at these crowds of Vanity's votaries, and to reflect how utterly frivolous and useless are all the objects of their lives—to think what an utter and appalling waste of life, and of all that should embellish and consecrate it—of youth and beauty and latent intellect—is scattered about these smothered and groaning counters. We never visit one of these establishments without feeling an almost uncontrollable desire to hang up the namby-pamby clerks by the heels, and send their customers home to cooking their dinners, or darning their husbands' hose.

Broadway, in its outward aspect, varies as much at different portions of the day as a fashionable lady. In the early morning it is quite hushed and solitary, and wears that air of indescribable and hopeless desolation which is encountered on the stage of a theatre after the performance is over, and the audience have taken their departure. You look around with a feeling of almost uneasiness. It does not seem possible that this is the noisy, rattling, bustling, flashing, joyous Broadway, to which your steps are accustomed. It is rather some Palmyra avenue, solemn and deserted, to which you have been Aladdinized. Soon, however, the sidewalks begin to fill with the clerks and early workers, trudging down town to begin their day—the awakened swine gallop furiously downward to have the first cut of the new garbage which, despite the City Fathers, is sure to have been deposited in the gutters—the omnibuses begin to sidle up conveniently to the curbstone, soliciting your "powerful patronage;" and a belated bill-sticker, tipsy from want of sleep, tries to rub off his paste-pot against your legs, in passing. In an hour or two the great thoroughfare will be alive, and the whole city will go surging and thundering through it—a human river in a freshet, roaring and foaming towards the sea.

To see Broadway in its glory, however, you must wait till six o'clock, P. M. Then, if you take your stand in the door of a shop on the "fashionable side," you will see New York's possible in the way of beautiful women, scrupulously-dressed dandies, and pretty children. It is only at this hour of the day that the distinction between the east and west side is imperative. In the morning, or at midday, if absolutely forced to go through Broadway, you may take the sidewalk most shady or convenient without positive loss of character. But at grand promenade hour, wo be to the unhappy wight or distressed damsel who should be seen plodding along the shilling pavement! This distinction is gradually lessening under the influence of Stewart's and other magnificent establishments recently erected on the prohibited side, and whose attractions are strong enough to compel the haughty procession of fashion to cross over. Still, however, it is extremely unsafe for any lady or gentleman with nothing but a fashionable reputation to lose, to make an appearance on the shilling side after five o'clock, post meridian.

We ought, in strict justice, to say something pungent and denunciatory about the wretched cobble-stone pavement of Broadway, which, although "taken up" three or four times a year, does not mend its ways. But, in mercy to the civil authorities and uncivil reporters, we forbear. As to the latter gentlemen, to deprive them of the pavement in Broadway as a subject for the exercise of their wits, would be literally taking the ground from under their feet. And, besides, the sight of the here-and-there patches of good, solid, smooth Russ pavement, puts us in a good humor with the present, and makes us hope for the future. We know that the fashionable ladies in the metropolis, who *must* take their afternoon drive in Broadway, are looking forward with intense expectation to this granite millennium; and we are equally certain that the worthy City Fathers, when they become aware of this, will push on the good work they have begun, and so relieve glorious Broadway from the inconvenient stigma of being built on both sides of an impassable gully.

[Thus had we written on Broadway, when a friend to whom we submitted it, broke out with the following apostrophe, which we took down in shorthand, and insert as a part of the " Slice."]

We could rail at you, Broadway, by the hour. What scamp, of "high or low degree"—what hard-hearted woman of fashion—what knavish politician—what pompous man of wealth—small official—blackleg—what painted bawd, or smooth-faced hypocrite—what idealess dandy or sickly girl of sentiment—in a word, what form of folly or crime have you not lent yourself to—made much of? Giving the benefit of your sunshine and promenade side to every one of them in their newest gloss. Oh, the villains thou hast entertained, Broadway! The men of pretence! newly-arrived Viscounts! returned exquisites! celebrities, notorieties, infamies of every color and degree! And yet, turning to the other side of the ledger, there is a large credit for thee, for thou hast shown us the great bearded Turk, John Chinaman, the Choctaw in his blanket, prophets, long-haired reformers, and whatever else of strange and wonderful in character the world could furnish. Thou hast the first of every thing—of a General returned from victory—of a night-procession with its flaming torches—the great funerals—it is you that open wide your arms, and give a welcome to great men from every quarter of the land. No matter what the complexion of their politics: it's all the same to you. You look with an equal pride, an equal smile of satisfaction, on Webster and Jackson, on Scott and Clay. Has any man ever undertaken to estimate the notabilities who have been irretrievably swallowed up in its ever-flowing wave? Of a few of the humbler, we can recollect within the few past years that dietetic phenomenon the gingerbread man, who, in spite of the energetic buttoning of his coat to the throat, and the enormous strides he was used to make, was overtaken and submerged. And Posthlewaite Page, the mighty calculator of the function of A in the tap of a beer-barrel as affecting the sidereal system, where is he? And Nazro, that modest inculcator of Hebrew at 100,000 doubloons per lesson? The long-bearded man with the inexhaustible long nine? And the whitewash man? Alas! these have all perished from the sight.

Strange to say, although this mighty medium for the exhibition of all that is singular and eccentric, Broadway cannot claim a single peculiarity for itself. There is not a single feature by which you can define it—no one quality by which it is distinguishable from the commonest street. You can say of it, it is a great sheet of glass, through which the whole world is visible as in a transparency. In fact, rest you content in New York, and, making a pilgrimage from time to time to this thoroughfare, we will engage you shall see, in due succession, whatever your heart is set on. The world will come to you from every part in Broadway. You have heard, perhaps, of an elephant in Siam of exceeding size, wonderful docility, the temper of an angel—you would give a finger to have a sight of him: one day a trumpet is blown, you prick up your ears, and making for Broadway, behold "Siam," just arrived, and marching in state at the head of a caravan.

The celebrated Musical College of *La Scala*, Milan, is in high enthusiasm with the singing of Signorina Luni. Shall we ever hear her? will her countrymen part with her? You fear, never. A turn of the wheel, and the Signorina is seen, through a coach-window, taking her first drive in America, in Broadway. So of dancers, jugglers, lords, marchionesses, panoramas, cosmoramas, dancing birds. In questions of apparel, Broadway has an equal variety and preference. If there's a peculiar hat born and worn in Bond-street, London; a new Revolutionary blouse in Paris; an extraordinary pair of trowsers in Berlin; or a special style of beard among the Persians; or Russian whiskers, or Roman moustache—in its season, and when each has attained its ripeness—look for it in Broadway, and you shall find it. The whole world, once in the course of its life, flocks to Broadway! and yet nothing sticks.

Trinity Church.

There is not in all Broadway a memorable building—(shall we except Trinity Church and Mr. Stewart's Dry Goods Store?)—not a monument—not a sight worth the seeing! Its chief characteristic is, that all things shall be brought to a certain well-bred and immovable level. Mark the passengers: not as the people, in other more Democratic precincts, scrambling freely about, dashing to right and left, taking across the way at an angle—but all moving in a right line, to the right up, to the right down. All dressed in about the same decent habiliments, all carrying heads up, and observing the decorum of the street with due gravity and steadiness. Broadway never, or rarely, has its gentlemanly propriety disturbed by the rush of a fire-engine, or a drove of cattle, or the tramp of a target excursion.

For real life, and the display of numbers, Broadway is in full force through Sunday, and with an increased power on Sunday evening. It is then that the nice dressing of New Yorkers is to be seen in the highest perfection—a solid mass from Grace Church to the Battery—a perfect Mississippi, with a double current up and down, of glossy broadcloth and unblemished De Laines. An army on the march to battle could not move with stricter precision—a procession of monks and nuns bound convent-ward, with more sacred gravity. New York in Broadway, on that day, makes a mighty sacrifice to solemnity, requiting itself a little in the evening by stepping aside into the shops and gardens, and rapping for innumerable ice-creams.

It is above all other streets, localities, and positions, the test of respectability. If you can touch your hat to fifty people in Broadway, your character is "O. K."—you are an established man. But beware of "cuts." They are dealt about in that thoroughfare with an awful profusion. If you are in doubt about yourself, if you are under a cloud, if your hat is rusty, or your coat "going," if you have been paragraphed as having failed, or as involved in any little unfortunate matter, shun Broadway as you would a fire. You will be shot down on your first appearance like an outlaw. You will not have a minute's mercy allowed you. You will not pass ten steps before some kind gentleman, suddenly oblivious of your countenance,

CHATHAM-SQUARE

will bring home to you painfully a sense of your miserable condition. Till Fortune befriend you, sneak through the side streets.

There are hundreds and thousands in New York who cannot live out of Broadway: who must breathe its air at least once in the day, or they gasp and perish. They are creatures of conventionality, whose sole luxury, whose chief enjoyment in this world, is to have certain hats touched to them every day of their life in Broadway. This is their morning's anticipation, their evening's reminiscence; and when at length they find this world and its affairs closing upon them, they call a confidential friend to their bedside, and whisper in his ear, as they are going, "Let the funeral go through Broadway!"

Slice II.—CHATHAM-STREET.

CHATHAM-STREET is undoubtedly the place where Swedenborg got his grand idea that the internal spirit gives form and aspect to the outward manifestation. Patched and threadbare walls, leaky roofs, low ceilings and narrow windows—squalid cellars, filthy holes and corners, back-doors that seem the entrances to dark caves—slovenly, hard-shelled women and sinister-looking men—skeleton show-windows, dropsical displays of rickety furniture and putrefying cast-off finery—reeking feather-beds, three-legged pine-tables and disjointed joint-stools—second-hand cooking-stoves, coats and castors, mud and mock-auctions,—these are some of the leading "constituent principles" of Chatham-street. One sees at a glance that here is the home and haunt of the shopkeeping, penny-turning genius, in its meanest and most grovelling manifestation. In some streets that we know of, one feels sometimes a little—a very little—surprised at being cheated if he makes a purchase; but when we arrive in Chatham-street we have left all that behind us. The only wonder is, shall we get out safely with our coat on—or shall we have traded it off for some villainous scoured-up concern a mile too big in the back, but which we have been convinced by the wheedling Israelite, fits us as if for a wedding?

Not that there are not honest shops—as shop-honesty goes in these days—in Chatham street—only they don't, somehow, seem to thrive, and we never heard of anybody happening to get into one of them. So that our classification—we beg that to be distinctly understood—leaves them out of the question.

The higgledy-piggledy which we enumerated at starting as being the general element of Chatham-street, naturally arranges itself into:

I. The Clothing Stores;
II. The Furniture and Pawnbroker establishments;
III. The Mock Auctions, Lottery Offices, Groggeries, &c., &c.

The Clothing Stores are invariably kept by Jews. A Yankee ('cute as they are) slop-keeper in Chatham-street could not exist—it is a physical impossibility. The Jew is gentle—he is insinuating—somewhat even polished; knows at a glance whether you are from the Country or the City, whether you have a monkeyish taste for finery and gewgaws, or want something rough and substantial. He is, too, a great artist, especially in coats. You may have experienced some difficulty and vexation in getting your tailor in Broadway to fit you? Pshaw! Step into the nearest clothing-store in Chatham-street and slip on a coat—*any* coat—and we'll wager our wedding-suit that it is a "shplendid fit." There is no such thing as an ill-fitting coat in Chatham-street. Every coat there fits everybody. After you get it home, your wife or friends may perhaps discover that it appears to have been made for the alderman of the ward. But, then, even that is a great deal better than if it had been too small. It can be easily taken in; and in fact, coming from Chatham-street, there is no wonder it took you in first.

If you would traffic in trowsers, you must, however, be a little more particular. The press-board has been placed across the back corner of the shop, by way of tiring-room; and there, behind a far perspective of dangling coat-skirts, you proceed to encase yourself in the unmentionables, once another's. Tender thought—and, alas! too often tender trowsers too! For, if by any possibility they should happen not to fit, the shopman will infallibly make you tear a tremendous chasm in them before you get them off, and there you have them on your——hands, we suppose we must say, although that doesn't exactly express the idea. The prices of clothing, in these establishments, are as varied as the sizes and dispositions of the customers. Most persons who trade there go prepared for a tremendous dicker; but the reality so far exceeds their anticipations that they generally "come down," and are contented to get off with a shave, the depth of which depends altogether on certain little things which we greatly fear will prevent General Cass being elected President. It is the sublimity of shopkeeping, the poetry of peculation. At first they troll you on, as it were, into an ambush from which there can be no possible escape. They will perhaps even agree with you a little, and admit, with seeming reluctance, your suggestion that a button is wanting here, or a redundancy should be suppressed there. Then, when you have exhausted your weapons; when you have said every thing you could think of in deprecation of the garment you are about to purchase; then watch well your shopkeeper! Then comes *his* turn; and, casting upon you some such scornful, pitying yet hungry glances, as Mr. Webster gave Mr. Haynes on the day he ate the Carolinian, he commences. He does not take you by storm—he uses no clap-trap—he despises all such vulgar auxiliaries. He has set himself to convince you out of your eyes and wheedle you out of your money—and this he will *do.* Before you have listened five minutes you are satisfied your case is gone. In another similar interval you begin to be convinced that it *does* fit like your skin; that the price is less than a quarter what it is worth; and that you were truly a fortunate man when you ventured into Chatham-street. We had intended to have reported one of these sartorian orations to you; but upon second thought, we have no right to spoil any man's business; and so you must go listen for yourself.

For the greater portion of Chatham-street these Clothing Stores line the southern sidewalk, without interruption; and the coat-tails and pantaloon-legs flap about the face of the pedestrian, like the low branches in a wood-path. In front of each, from sunrise to sundown, stands the natty, black-bearded and fiercely-moustached proprietor; every now and then venturing, when a countryman passes, to tap him delicately on the arm, and invite him to look at the "magnificent assortment" of wares and wearables within. Stooping, as you enter the low, dark doorway, you find yourself in the midst of a primitive formation of rags, carefully classified into vests, coats, and pantaloons, and each neatly labelled. In fact, it would require no great stretch of the imagination to fancy yourself in a cabinet of carefully preserved raimental antiquities—with this exception: that the philosopher in attendance seems rather willing to sell his "specimens," which the Farmers' Club, we are certain, would not do.

The expertness acquired by the keepers of these shops in "spotting" their man is truly wonderful. They know a greenhorn from the country by instinct; and there is something almost beautiful in the certainty with which they pounce upon him and the tenacity with which they cling to him. No matter what he wants, or whether he wants any thing—they are sure to fit him and to trade with him. If he won't buy new clothes, they will sell him old ones; nay, they will swap with him for any thing he has on, from hat to boots—always managing to get a little something "to boot," and to send him off fully impressed with the idea that he is not only the best dressed but the best-looking man in the City. If his toggery, however, holds together till he gets home, he may account himself a fortunate individual; and if it don't, what is he to do about it? There is no use in talking about trading back. Oh yes—they are all politeness, and perfectly willing to trade back—but let him beware! Every swap he makes will be sure to leave him worse off than before. He had better reconcile himself to "circumstances," and mind to keep out of Chatham-street for the future.

The Furniture and Pawnbroking establishments in Chatham-street are not less worthy of attention than the Clothing Stores. If one would know the ultimatum of the Rickety, let him buy a lot of furniture in Chatham-street. We have often seen a furniture-car laden with this sort of truck moving through the street, leaving a broad wake behind of chair-legs and table-leaves, which had been jolted out of their proper places and fallen overboard. And we once heard of an old lady who, being somewhat tired and fleshy, undertook to ride home in a four-dollar rocking-chair which she had just purchased. But alas! upon reaching her own door, she had become a fixture. The chair, upon being exposed to the weather, had shrunk so rapidly as to fasten her immediately in one of the joints. She was rescued with great difficulty—but the chair never recovered.

These establishments are much frequented by economical housekeepers afflicted with that most melancholy of all distempers, a mania for cheap bargains; and many a dollar is paid for "cheap" articles, which in a few weeks become utterly and irrecoverably useless, while the deluded purchaser is congratulating herself upon the excellent bargain she has made. The Auctions, too, for secondhand furniture are another *furore* for the bargain-hunter; and here the most incredible swindles are daily and hourly enacted, with varnished bureaus, cracked crockery, and asthmatic bedsteads. Carpets that have been trampled under foot nearly as long as the Irish peasantry, are here pushed off at the price of new, and feather-beds filled with shavings, are bid off at rates that would purchase wholesome and comfortable mattresses. In short, Chatham-street may well be denominated the gathering-place of gullibility, the metropolis or shams. There is nothing real, reliable, or valuable about it. The whole business is a miserable speculating, under the pretence of cheap utility, upon the avarice, the weakness, and the ignorance of its customers. The very cheapness which is its strongest recommendation, ought to be a sufficient proof that there must be a lie somewhere in the business. Common sense will tell any man, or woman either, that what cannot be purchased at a respectable shop for less than twenty dollars, cannot be sold in Chatham-street for ten. But common sense has very little to do with those who make purchases in Chatham-street; and it would seem that the main purpose of their lives and adventures is to illustrate and embellish the coarse but pregnant truth, that "a fool and his money are soon parted."

Of the Pawnbrokers' shops we have elsewhere spoken. They are not confined to Chatham-street, nor are they always indicated by the three golden balls. There is scarcely a second-rate jewelry-shop or exchange-office in the City that is not, to a greater or less extent, a Pawnbroking establishment; and it is probable that these places are the repositories of a greater number and variety of the dramas enacted in the world of poverty and crime, than all the police-offices or charity-hospitals in the country.

Slice III.—WALL-STREET.

We are conscious of a double sensation as we write the words—one of descending motion, when we think of all the million deceits and degradations and hypocrisies and miseries played off there as in some ghostly farce; another, proud and elevating, in thus taking familiarly on the point of our pen the great purse-string of America—the key of the Union. As money rules the world, so Wall-street rules money; and from its dingy dens go forth the mandates which make plenty or misery, peace or war, and stamp the whole character of the nation and the destiny of its people. It may have been thought strange by many small victims and outsiders, that we passed over Wall-street while treating of the gambling-houses of the metropolis. Not so. It is true that gambling is carried on as the chief business there; but it is upon so gigantic, so systematic a scale, that it reaches the dignity of history. It rather deserves a place in our history of revolutions.

Wall-street! Who shall fathom the depth and the rottenness of thy mysteries? Has Gorgon passed through thy winding labyrinth, turning with his smile every thing to stone—hearts as well as houses? Art thou not the valley of riches told of by the veracious Sindbad, where millions of diamonds lay glistening like fiery snow, but which was guarded on all sides by poisonous serpents, whose bite was death and whose contact was pollution?

Let us look from the front of this lofty temple to God, down Wall-street—what do we see? Nothing but a dim confusion—a turbid stream of

WALL-STREET

painful, intertwisted motion, rolling and chafing between gray stone banks on either side. That is all there is of Wall-street—absolutely nothing but some heaps of granite, as they might be mole-hills, with men running about like pismires, in and out, and about and about.

But let us look again. Wall-street, after all, can't be so dreadful a place as all this comes to. You must at least admit that it has set the town a noble example of what ought to be done in the way of architecture. Whatever may be its faults—and doubtless it has as many of them as a pretty woman—it is beyond all odds the handsomest street on the continent. In the length of half a mile from the Custom-House there is a greater amount and variety of architectural taste than in many an entire city. The Custom-House itself is a grand structure, quite worthy of being the central gate, as it were, of the gigantic commerce that pours through it the wealth and luxury of the world, to be distributed in a thousand avenues through a rich and prosperous empire, inhabited by twenty millions of extravagant people. This edifice, with its busy yet quiet inmates, will, perhaps, one day claim our especial notice. At present we will pass down its interminable steps, reminding one of the descent from the Pyramid Gizeh; and, stumbling over a row of learned canary-birds, pitching into a repository of carving-knives, and upsetting a kennel of young puppies, pursue our way. On either side the street presents a graceful and broken line of classic fronts and Grecian porticoes, of lofty steps and dizzy colonnades. It would seem as if we had found an avenue of temples—and so we have: only they are all erected to one divinity and devoted to the worship of one god—Mammon. Midway stands the massive Exchange, looking as if it had been hewed out of a solid granite mountain. It is supported on one side by the inevitable fancy soap and shaving-cream man, and on the other by an oyster-wagon. Up its steep steps and through its labyrinthine halls and chambers, rush ever an eager throng of men, as if they went whirling about in some gigantic puppet-show, while a concealed hand pulled convulsively at the wire. Within the innermost range of columns, we push open a massive door and enter the Rotunda—almost a Coliseum in its magnitude and spacious proportions, and in every way a perfect work of art. This is the very sanctuary of Trade and Commerce, those Titanic powers which rule the world. But they must only be glanced at to-day. To examine and describe in detail what is taking place here would detain us too long from our walk. A thousand busy beings are in humming motion and activity within these walls; and upon the low, half-uttered, half-indicated dialogues going on, the wealth or poverty of hundreds of thousands—the price of stocks, the quotations of flour and cotton, the plenty or scarcity of money—all will be decided. In such a scene as this the mere operations of the money-making faculty lose the commonplaceness of their character, and become almost poetical and sublime. This is the heart of trade—and such a heart!

On the southern corner stand a half-score or so of excited faces, many of them with the Israelitish nose so proverbial for smelling out a good thing in embryo or a bad one just beginning to taint. These are the famous Third Board—mostly lame ducks who have been disabled for life in their passage through the more secret operations of the regular Board up-stairs, and greenhorns who are very anxious to come in and be caught. They are at present unable to deal in realities, or "Fancies" either, but they still take the keenest interest in what transpires in the former field of their labors, and in brisk and animated discussions of the prices and prospects of stocks, seem to derive a melancholy pleasure in "fighting their battles o'er again." Poor fellows! While gravely debating questions of millions, many of them would find a most inconvenient tightness in the money market if they were to attempt treating themselves to a shilling stew.

It is now high tide in Wall-street. Every cellar vomits its pale young man with calf-skin memorandum-book, griped firmly as he hurries away to one of the innumerable Banks, or swallows some wild-looking "short," who rushes down and hysterically inquires of his obliging neighbor, Mr. Smith, whether he hasn't a few hundred over. It is half-past two o'clock, and the crisis is fast coming on! From cellar to cellar he speeds as if he bore the blazing brand of Roderick Dhu, and feared that it would go out before it had performed its mission. No help! no help! everybody seems, strangely enough, as short as himself. In thirty minutes, he, who yesterday commanded his thousands, will be ruined and a beggar—a mark set upon him which will forever debar him from gaining credit there again. He sees passing in swift perspective his splendid establishment Above Bleecker given up to the hands of the Sheriff—his heartless wife and spendthrift daughters loading him with complaints and reproaches at his altered state—his friends one by one deserting him—his position lost, and himself an outcast. Who wonders that, in a moment of despair, he seizes whatever is left him, defrauds his creditors of his remaining assets, and elopes, or—a still more quiet and gentlemanly way—applies a razor to the jugular, and thus frees himself at once of earthly ills?

But hark! The clock strikes three. As if by magic, the bustle and confusion which but now ran through the street, ceases, and the whole neighborhood rapidly subsides into the calm of Sabbath. Stillness reasserts her empire. Wall-street is locked up and gone home for the day. The omnibuses in Broadway expand with their double fares—many even mount the step, preferring the chance of being thrown off, or rubbed off against a cab, or splashed deplorably; and the whole living scene disappears—leaving nothing but the gray stone walls and irregular pavements, and innumerable tin signs, of all that which was so lately noisy and lively Wall-street.

Slice IV.—THE TOMBS.

Grim mausoleum of hope! Foul lazar-house of polluted and festering Humanity! A chill and noisome blast, as the midnight breath of graveyards, salutes us as we enter beneath thy frowning vestibule—a bitter wind, laden with groans and imprecations, hurrying swiftly away frightened at what it has seen and heard, and hastening to lose itself in the purifying sunshine of the upper world. What unsightly labyrinths of filth and abomination—what heaped-up cells of iniquity and unrepentant crime—what dens of drunken madness, howling over the grave of Reason—what dark recesses, sacred to the orgies of a corrupt and abominable Justice—hast thou not passed over! No wonder that thou art tainted with a poison that strikes to the very soul but to breathe. No wonder that in such a redhot furnace of corruption, bribery, theft, burglary, murder, prostitution, and delirium tremens, the very air is rarefied with crime. We can hardly realize that there is in the whole gloomy edifice an honest space whereon a man may safely set his foot. Where, then, shall we begin—on the Bench, or in the Cell? At the Law, or its Victims? In the Bar, or the Dungeon? No matter where. Let us enter by a side door, and explore from the ground upward.

It is within an hour of daylight. A Policeman stands at the low door, and seeing that we are "connected with the press," offers no obstacle to our entrance.—Sometime he may have a "case" which he has been paid for suppressing—and then we may be of use to him. We enter and grope our way with difficulty, stumbling here and there over a sleeping Watchman, and making slowly towards a dim and distant glimmering light. Approaching, we see a dark-lantern held so that its single ray may illuminate the corrugated face and ghastly spectacles of the Police Magistrate who is doing up the loafers and loaferesses in squads. The recesses of the damp unwholesome apartment are filled with drunken men and women found helpless in the street, with night-brawlers and disturbers of the public peace, and with young boys and girls who have been caught asleep on cellar doors or are suspected of the horrible crime of stealing junk bottles and old iron!—The very lowest and most brutal form of human depravity may here be seen in all its horrors; and the most horrible sight of all is the blear-eyed, drunken woman, arrested for robbing her paramour or for quarrelling with her companions on the Points, and waiting her turn, among negro men and women, thieves and vagabonds, of every age and quality, to be "taken care of," in that tender and affectionate manner in which Society is in the habit of providing for such of her children as cannot take care of themselves. Our Magistrate has work enough to provide all these unfortunates with comfortable quarters, either on Blackwell's Island or in the Drunkards' Room, and it is necessary that he should begin betimes, and proceed by summary measures. As each case is called, the Watchman on whose list it is, comes forward, gives a wink at a worm-eaten Bible on the desk, and proceeds to relate his side of the story. This is all that the Magistrate has time to listen to. The miserable creature who has fallen into the Watchman's clutches is at once committed and hurried away. If he has money, he may manage well enough with the Watchman, and make his escape at once. But if not, he must go to quod and wait next day for the visits of the "shyster" lawyers—a set of turkey-buzzards, whose touch is pollution and whose breath is pestilence. If the prisoner, however, has neither money nor friends, Justice is rigid and uncompromising. No Shyster disturbs his drunken meditations and no Keeper alleviates the agonies of returning sobriety. Thrown howling and infuriated into a yard filled with wretches like himself, they aid each other's attempts at demonism, until the whole place becomes a shuddering Hell. The women are crammed into a long lampless corridor, and lie huddled up in their rags against the bare stone walls, or rave in hideous fury to and fro, until their strength is exhausted and they fall prone upon the floor.

This is the mere fancy-work of the Tombs. Later in the morning the real business of the day begins up-stairs. The "Judge," as the understrappers of the office and the Reporters always take care to style him, has taken his seat, with a well-blanked Clerk on either side. And now, open the doors of your cages, worthy Policemen, and drive your wild animals into the ring! Here they come! An appalling company, glaring upon us with ferocious eyes, or livid as the hue of death. Save the outline, not a ray nor trace of humanity can we discover in them all. Driven by remorseless hunger or despair, or the goadings of unnatural and consuming appetites, they have debauched every human feeling and instinct out of their very being. Full half of them are women, and, with the exception that they are charged with graver offences, the present company, both male and female, are for the most mere counterparts of the gang we saw at daybreak, and are sent off, one after another, to await their trial at the Court of Sessions.—Occasionally, however, a well-dressed swindler who has robbed his employer or forged his friend's name, or a still handsome woman of the town, may be seen in the public dock. But generally, all such are able, in one way or another, to secure an examination in the private room, or as the indignant Reporters (when they are not permitted to share the spoils) term it, the "Star Chamber." In this room, Justice transacts business upon a splendid scale. Every thing is acceptable, and nothing comes amiss, from the cool thousand in veritable mopusses, to the canary-bird or the broadcloth cloak of some poor devil, hitherto "respectable," but who has blundered into an unsuccessful speculation. Here, too, the handsome and dashing Cyprians who have been complained of for "touching" a country merchant, a parish clergyman, or a green Congressman on his way home, receive the honors of a private examination before the "Judge" himself. By the way, our country friends, the merchant, clergyman, and Congressman aforesaid, will bear us out in the assertion that these cases generally terminate with the arrest of the frail deceiver, and the announcement, on the part of the sympathizing officer, that "the money has not been recovered." Sometimes, if the amount is large, and a "muss" would perhaps lead to inconvenient investigations, the victim gets half of it back again, out of which he gladly pays that "indefatigable and efficient officer, A. B. C. D. E. F. G. Smith," five dollars for his trouble, and sneaks off about his business.

People are apt to imagine that a thief, or a woman who robs a rich customer, makes thriving business of it; but they do not know all. The drawbacks and discounts to which a poor thief is subjected before being permitted to get clear of the Tombs with his prey, are a very serious and ruinous reduction of his profits. What with the sub-rosa lion's slice for the ——, the gratuity to the attentive clerks, and the open bribery to the officers and reporters, (the latter only admitted in case of respectability and social position,) we think, after all, that we had rather be a member of the "Exterior Board" in Wall-street than a genteel thief.

If you would know what is the extreme of human degradation and misery, visit the Tombs, and take a walk through its various ranges of cells, and apartments. You may, perhaps, not be especially shocked at the condition of the inmates of the cells along the more aristocratic corridors, where the forgers, murderers, and genteel swindlers are confined. They are allowed bed-linen and books, and may, if they choose, keep themselves cleanly and comfortable. But wait! Let us open this great gate, and step into the cattle-yard, where are herded the miserable wretches who have been found guilty of drunkenness and starvation! Or, if you still survive, let us go into the female department, and hear the drunken, bloated, diseased white and black women cursing and blaspheming! Then remember that all these monstrous creatures were born with pure, beautiful womanly souls, and that the chances are nine hundred and ninety-nine in a thousand that they were driven to their present condition by starvation and the wiles of some heartless man-villain, and that they alone are punished while the man goes free—and you have humanity before you in its most demoniac aspect, its most revolting manifestation.

As to the "judiciary" of this celebrated establishment, very little can be said—for we have no inclination to share the hospitalities of the polite prison-keeper for the heinous and unpardonable sin of Contempt of Court. In truth the Judges, or more properly speaking, the Police Justices, are generally honest and vigilant officers, and discharge their duties conscientiously and fearlessly. The Watch and Police departments we have already described; therefore, with a few words of deserved eulogy upon the Court of Quarter Sessions and the great and good man who presides over its deliberations with equal dignity and intelligence, politeness and impartiality, and whose judicial decisions have already been the themes of admiration upon the tongues of unborn millions, we shall beg leave to bid adieu to the dingy precincts of the Tombs—never to return to them if we can help it. It is true that there are not wanting detractors from the fair fame of this distinguished head of American jurisprudence, who deny his eloquence, and even go the length of impugning his parts of speech! But what great man ever existed exempt from calumny? Even Bonaparte has his revilers; and there are wretches in existence who deny the reality of the Fejee mermaid. It is true that there are very strong complaints made of the manner in which criminal justice is administered in this Court; but we venture to say that they are altogether unfounded.

Slice V.—THE FIVE POINTS.

TURNING eastwardly from the Tombs into a street that would strike even the practised eyes and hardened olfactories of a veteran New-Yorker as particularly foul and loathsome, a few steps bring us to the great central ulcer of wretchedness—the very rotting Skeleton of Civilization, whence emanates an inexhaustible pestilence that spreads its poisonous influence through every vein and artery of the whole social system, and supplies every heart-throb of metropolitan life with a pulse of despair. No matter how hopeful a soul you may bring with you into these horrible precincts, it will be many hours after you have left them before your mind can regain its temper. The memory of the horrors that here breed and gender will haunt you like a fiend, forbidding hope for a human nature that may become thus degraded.

Mere words can convey but a faint idea of the Five Points; but what can be thus accomplished has been so well done already by Dickens and Willis that we hesitate to attempt going over the same ground. But no description of New York, no matter how discursive or superficial, could pass over this, one of its most prominent and revolting features. As in most other cases, the architectural aspect of the place is a striking indication of its character and purposes. The Five Points lies in the bottom of the Delta-valley formed by the divergence of Centre and Chatham streets, and receives its name from the five corners or points where Anthony-street, coming from the west, and Orange from the north, intersect, and are cut through by Cross-street, running from the Tombs eastwardly to Mott-street. The buildings in all that neighborhood are nearly all of wood, and are so old and rotten that they seem ready to tumble together into a vast rubbish-heap. Many of them are furnished with steps, from which half the stairs are missing, and each provided with a decayed cellar-door, broken from the hinges, and ready to precipitate any one who ventures to tread upon it into the cellar below. Nearly every house and cellar is a groggery below and a brothel above. In the doors and at the windows may be seen at any hour of the afternoon or evening, scores of sluttishly-dressed women, in whose faces drunkenness and debauchery have destroyed every vestige of all we expect in the countenance of Woman, and even almost every trace of human expression. They are of all colors, white, yellow, brown, and ebony black; and from house to house, from cellar to cellar, and across the narrow street, flows a continuous stream of obscenity and blasphemy, which makes the very soul shudder. Here and there, digging in the foul gutters, or basking in filthy nakedness upon the cellar doors, may be seen groups of children, from the merest infancy up to the verge of premature puberty—some seeming pretty, some deformed and idiotic, and others horribly ulcerated from head to foot with that hereditary leprosy which debauchery and licentiousness entail as their curse upon their innocent offspring. Oh God! that helpless and unconscious infancy should thus come into this sorrowful world with its innocent veins filled with corruption instead of blood, and its tender body given over to the cancerous vulture of incurable disease even from its mother's womb!—And this not once in a great ways, but constantly recurring—scores, ay, hundreds and hundreds of them crowded into the space of a single neighborhood—born, living, and dying amid sores and vermin, never seeing nor hearing from the cradle to the grave aught of pure or innocent save the sky so far beyond their reach and the wind that gets astray in these frightful realms and sighs as it flees away. Is it any wonder that we have so many cases of "juvenile depravity" reported in the newspapers?

But let us enter one of these dark abodes. We have taken the precaution of getting ourselves accompanied by an officer, and the blear-eyed inmates of the "crib," both male and female, receive us with some show of reluctant civility. It is in the afternoon, and many of the inhabitants and frequenters are absent. The reception-room is furnished with wooden benches, and one corner is garnished with a bar, behind which, barricaded with broken-lipped bottles and sixpenny tumblers, stands the bloated mistress of the house, ready to administer drugged brandy at any price from three cents to a dollar a glass, according to the stage of intoxication at which the customer has arrived. Half a dozen disgusting wretches who ought to be women, are lounging upon the benches in immodest attitudes, while others gather about you, and insist upon your "treating," as they "haven't had a drop all day." The officer seems to be an old acquaintance; and they at first played shy, until he assured them that this time his visit was not a hostile one. Passing through the house, we stumble down three or four rickety steps and enter a still meaner and more squalid building in the rear, with only six feet space between the two. Here all is silent, and we see no one. A heap of rags, however, stirs in the corner, and examining more nearly, there appears a female face, ghastly with suffering, the eyes glassy as if set in death. Even while we gaze, the jaw falls, and, with a gurgling imprecation, the spirit of the prostitute seeks its Maker. What a death-bed! What an awful entrance to the world of immortal justice!

Clambering with difficulty up a narrow staircase, leading from the room where the stranger's hand has closed the eyes of the poor erring, suffering sister, we enter an apartment separated by tattered blankets, suspended from the low rafters, and inhabited by several families. Here a mother lies dead-drunk in her squalid bed upon the floor, and her two children are fighting over her body for the bottle which she may not have drained quite to its dregs. There two women, their eyes inflamed and their faces distorted with passion, are swearing furiously at each other, and threatening a war of blows. Yonder, on a cot without mattress or pillow, lies a paralytic old woman, looking as if living and malignant eyes had been given to a decaying wax-figure.—Our companion tells us that she has lain in that place, and in nearly the same condition, more than a quarter of a century, praying for death—cursing for death—blaspheming for death to come and end her earthly sufferings. Once she was beautiful and joyous and innocent, and her voice rang and her eye flashed gladness around her path. She had a husband, too, and a darling daughter. Her husband was poor, while she had been bred in splendor and extravagance. The girlish romance, in the height of which she had eloped with her poor lover, subsided in a year; in another, the hero-lover had become the hated husband. Her passion for dress and admiration, subdued so long, broke out afresh and with tenfold force. The rich lecher, on the hunt for spoils, found her, and she became a willing victim to vanity more than lust. She was beautiful and fascinating, and her paramour desired her all to himself. There is a break in the history here. But at any rate, her husband disappeared, and she dashed out into a brief season of guilty pleasure. Some said the poor man had been murdered, and others that he had drowned himself. But nobody ever made any discoveries—or if they did, they were bought off. The woman was deserted in a few months—who *could* be faithful to such a monster?—and fell rapidly through all the stages of prostitution, to end her miserable career amid the tortures and haunting memories of a living death. Such, in brief words, is one of the ten thousand heart-rending histories of the Five Points.

But we must descend to the street. It is night, and the thick and putrid atmosphere of the place is here and there illuminated by a sickly lamp, while the street begins to fill with rowdies, negroes, drunken sailors, pickpockets, burglars, and vagabonds of every description. It is Thursday night, and a grand "tear" is to be held in that large and rather aristocratic-looking cellar across the way. We will be on hand. Pah! what an intolerable stench of brandy, tobacco, and steaming carcasses, meets us at the top of the steps! But never mind; we have undertaken to see the Five Points, and we must not stop at trifles.

The room looks like a large, dimly-lighted cavern.—On a barrel by the side of the bar sits an old negro, tuning his fiddle, while the dancers on the floor have just taken their places. Away they go—a fat and shiny blackamore with his arm around the waist of a slight young girl, whose skin is yet white and fair, but whose painted cheeks and hollow glaring eyes tell how rapidly goes on the work of disease and death. Opposite this couple, a man naked as at the first moment of his birth, whirls shouting and yelling away with a brutal-looking woman, once evidently a queenly beauty. The other places in the cotillion are occupied by a notorious kracksman with his "pal"—a celebrated "toucher"—both of whom give our friend the officer a good-natured oath and a wink of recognition, and a stupid-looking sailor, more than half seas over, carefully watched by the hag who is to pick his pockets, and who never loses sight for an instant of her prey. Around the sides of the room in bunks, or sitting upon wooden benches, the remainder of the company wait impatiently their turn upon the floor—meanwhile drinking and telling obscene anecdotes, or singing fragments of ribald songs. This is the great Dance-house of the Five Points; and we have now seen enough.

Glad at length to escape from all these horrors, we hasten away, asking of ourselves, how is such a neighborhood kept up, and from what sources are the ranks of its female population recruited? But this touches the whole question of licentiousness and its causes, which we have left ourselves no room to discuss in the present number.

Slice VI.—THE GAMBLING-HOUSES.

We hope the respectable merchants and ambitious clerks who are in the habit of ordering supper in a private room at Delmonico's three nights in the week, for the purpose of playing brag at ten dollars *ante*, will not be alarmed at the title of our article. We do not by any means include Delmonico's among the gambling-houses, on account of such things being done in its private rooms. There is certainly no more entirely respectable and correctly-managed public-house in the country than Delmonico's; but how is a landlord to know—or how can he possibly interfere with—what is done quietly by his guests in the privacy of their rooms? If Delmonico's were to be censured for this, we know of plenty of private residences "above Bleecker," with freestone fronts and real silver bell-pulls, that would come under the ban directly. But it is not with the private gamblers that we have now to do. Invulnerable to the law, they escape even the long-reaching fingers of the press, and are secure from all rebuke save that of God and their own consciences—and perhaps now and then a beggared wife and family. There are more of them than anybody knows of; and if chamber-doors were made of glass, some people who are considered patterns of punctuality and models of financial propriety, would appear to very great disadvantage on 'Change; and there would be as great a revolution among "good names" in Bank as among the blouses in Paris. But, as we said, not a word of all that.

We will begin, however, at the Clubs. These, although assuming to be private, are in fact but too public, in the influence they exert over the minds and habits of the young, by placing dissipation and gambling in their most seductive and "respectable" aspects, and making high-spirited young men ambitious to be ruined. It is one of the perhaps incurable social evils of a political democracy, that it inspires men just entering into life in moderate circumstances, and with fair prospects, with an inextinguishable passion for *shining,* at any cost, even that of honor and reputation. Taught from childhood that all men are equal, and as they grow up seeing this doctrine practically carried out at the polls, (but nowhere else,) and incessantly talked about in the newspapers, they forget or overlook the great fact that *social* distinctions are as broad and well defined in this country as anywhere else in the world; and that the attempt of a young man whose fortune and position are yet to be made, to force himself into the society, upon equal terms, of the established and wealthy, must lead to speedy and inevitable ruin. The successful merchant or banker whose income is ten or twenty thousand dollars a year, is not necessarily compromised by losing a few hundreds at faro or brag, or by expending now and then an extra thousand upon a fashionable mistress. While the poor clerk, fired with the ambition of not being outshone by his associates, and proud of being admitted to their society, finds his paltry salary soon expended, and rushes headlong into debt and dishonor—ending too often, in crime and a prison.

The literal translation of "club" is "gambling-house." Nor does a club differ in any essential respect from a public rendezvous of this kind, except in the fact that in the former the business of plucking the pigeons and "putting through" the greenhorns is done by the "respectable" members, while in the latter it is confined to professed blacklegs. In the club as in the gambling-house, you have hot suppers and cool wines, jovial association, and the most seductive freedom of manners. In both, the pretence is pleasure, and the business gaming. But the club is more aristocratic, and more desirable to an ambitious young man, as being a fancied means of somehow (he doesn't exactly know how) elevating his social position, and giving him the *entrée* to good society—a pleasant dream which he never lives to see realized. The wives and daughters of the aristocratic members despise the club from the bottom of their hearts, and with very good reason, too. It is, of all devices for desolating the domestic circle, narrowing the affections, and driving Woman to that course of independent action ever fatal to her delicacy, if not her purity, the most pernicious and comprehensive in its influence. "The *habituée* of a club," said a married lady to us the other day, "can scarcely by any possibility be a good father, a good husband, or a good neighbor."

But we were about to speak especially of the gambling-houses—existing in open defiance of the laws, and with as little real concealment as the coffee-houses or oyster-cellars. The public know all about them, where they are, who manage them, and who are their regular frequenters. Once in a while, to save appearances, some establishment is complained of, and, perhaps, tried and convicted. The keeper pays five hundred or a thousand dollars, by way of fine or gratuity,—Justice is satisfied, and the business goes on. This has been and always must be the case until we can have a City Government composed of men who have no party pledges to fulfil, no political ambition to gratify, no hungry pockets to feed with bribes. When will that be?

If you wish to visit a first-rate gambling-house, you had better make the acquaintance of some gentlemanly blackleg—"sporting-man" is the title by which he prefers to be known in his profession—and put yourself under his "protection." If this is not convenient, however, it will make no particular difference. Walk down by yourself, any time after ten o'clock at night, to one of the finest-looking houses in Park-place, and ring the bell. A colored gentleman will open the door; and, if you proceed as if you know what you are about, he will take it for granted that it is all right, and will immediately disappear, leaving you to make your own way. You open the door of the parlor on the right hand, and saunter carelessly in, probably meeting one of the proprietors, who asks you, in a tone of perfect and unobtrusive hospitality, if you will take supper. You generally decline; but on this particular occasion you may sit down at a luxuriously-furnished table, and mention to the waiter, who is instantly at your side, what you would like. You need not hesitate to consult your finest tastes. Game, according to the season, of every variety, and exquisitely cooked; the rarest French *entremets*—any thing, in short, you have a fancy for, will be instantly forthcoming. A bottle of iced champagne—the genuine Heidsic—is at your elbow; and if you have a fancy for a glass of rare Burgundy, or old South-side Madeira, you have only to make it known, and you will be supplied directly.

Having supped leisurely, for which remember you are to pay nothing, (unless you choose to "try your luck" a-fighting the tiger,) you saunter leisurely into the other parlor, where a group of fifteen or twenty—seldom more, except during the races, and other times of unusual excitement—is gathered about a "long, low, black" table, in the centre of which is a cloth containing, separately fastened down by the backs, all the cards of the "full deck." At one end of the table is seated a little crooked man, with fingers like eagle's claws, who has a little tin box before him, from which mysteriously slips one card at a time, which he lays on one of two piles, which grow impartially by alternate distribution beneath his hand. Every card that is dealt occasions a commotion, and a great change of places among sundry heaps of large ivory buttons—some white, some red—lying promiscuously about on the stationary cards on the table. You see no money, except now and then, when one of the players is "broke," he passes a V or an X up to the dealer, and receives its equivalent in buttons. The white ones count one dollar apiece, and the red ones five; so that you can readily see how easy it is for a man with a bad run of luck to lose several hundred dollars in the course of an evening.

And thus the game goes on, from night till gray morning—the pallid, eager, dull, beaming, reckless, and despairing faces gathered around the table, presenting a panorama of human passions, which it is interesting yet painful to contemplate. This is the very inner shrine of the temple of Mammon; and the devotees you see here are actuated solely by the simple, undisguised, almost demoniac, love of money. No scene nor phase of unadulterated human selfishness is below or beyond this. The robber who stabs his victim to get at his pocket—the incendiary who fires a city in the hope of spoils—is not more the slave of the lust for gold than that gray-headed sinner, or that bright-eyed, nervous youth, who stands leaning over the faro-table, watching every card as if the destiny of his immortal soul hung—and so perhaps it does—upon the issue.

Besides the halfscore tip-top concerns, of which we have attempted to give some general idea, there are in New York at least a hundred gambling-shops of lower grades, where the business is carried on upon a gradually reduced scale until you reach the Five Point negro-cellar, with its tallow candle stuck in a bottle, its pine table surrounded by grinning ebony faces mingled with white ones, like the men on a checker-board, when the fight rages hottest. These shops may generally be found in top garrets or back cellars, up blind alleys, and in all sorts of unexpected places. If your pockets want cleaning out, however, and you do not readily stumble over one of these dens, give the first watchman you meet a dollar, tell him your wants, and you will be soon provided. To gain admission here, no ceremony is necessary. Walk in without embarrassment, you are sure of being welcome—that is, provided you bring a reasonable amount of cash with you. Without this you would be like Grimalkin without claws in a place where the thermometer seldom gets below "spirits boil."

The room is small, dimly lighted, and meanly furnished; and around the table are gathered a group of men in whom all the higher and nobler attributes of humanity are wanting, and whose fierce eyes and savage faces are lit up with the most diabolical expression of intense and utter selfishness. Not one redeeming ray of superior intelligence or feeling ever gleams athwart those hateful and revolting countenances. The believer in human nature has here his benevolent creed put to the severest test. There is not a man in the company who does not appear capable of every crime; and the only evidence of humanity is an expression of super-brutal cunning, rendering them as dangerous of executing their schemes against society as reckless in conceiving them.

Gambling is the synthesis of crime, and includes within itself the spirit of fraud, theft, robbery, and murder. The professed gambler is the most enormous pest ever engendered by a monstrous society; and the neophyte, or the well-advanced disciple is dangerous and abhorrent, in the exact degree of his progress towards the finished sportsman. To the gambler, such other crimes as seduction, libertinism, and swindling, are mere amusement and leisure-play. All affections and noble instincts, all honor and just ambition, in him are extinguished by a ferocious insanity for money as insatiable and as ungovernable as the desires of a maniac or the fury of a beast. Men who have fallen under the control of this horrid vice should unquestionably be treated as the most dangerous of madmen, and should be securely confined, out of the reach of society.

In order to decoy victims into their snares, the gamblers have a regular system of police established upon all new-comers to the city, whose business it is to watch the arrivals at the hotels, and ascertain who among them are likely subjects to be operated upon. The spies employed in this business are often men of considerable address, and make a flashy-genteel appearance, very impressive and taking with greenhorns. The principal means of leading strangers into the trap are an introduction to the innumerable houses of ill-fame, the inmates of all of which are connected with one or the other of the gambling-houses. The decoy knows how to make himself agreeable to the stranger; points out the various curiosities of the City, supplies him with information respecting the various localities; tells him where the Postoffice, the Exchange, the Customhouse, &c. &c., can be found; and makes himself useful in a variety of ways. At evening they adjourn to the bar, fortify themselves with a julep, and by the time it is scientifically imbibed, Mr. Greenhorn is ripe for any thing. A walk is proposed; and in the course of a lounge on the Battery, or a saunter up Broadway, the City gentleman meets a female acquaintance, splendidly dressed, and uncommonly sociable—and condescending. Mr. Greenhorn is at once introduced, and the lady politely invites both gentlemen to call round in the course of the evening and see her. The countryman is delighted with such an unusual exhibition of hospitality, and begins to think New York a leetle the cutest place anywhere this side of sundown. Once fairly in the harlot's den, and his fate is sealed. Bewildered with the strangeness of all he sees and hears, overcome by flattery and attentions, he does not refuse a glass of champagne, which is drugged with a small quantity of morphine, just enough to inspire self-confidence and audacity; and the spy finds no difficulty in leading a willing victim to the gambling-house, where he is scientifically plucked, and left to make his way to his hotel, a ruined, miserable man.

Going still another step downward in our researches, we come upon the penny poker dens of the thieves and negroes of the Five Points, and other similar localities. These are indescribably filthy and abominable holes, into which a man with healthy lungs might penetrate with about as much safety as he would go down a well with an air-damp at the bottom. Here the various grades of small thieves and pickpockets may be seen, huddled together over a dark table, shuffling a pack of greasy and wornout cards, drinking villainous brandy and fire-new whiskey—swearing, quarrelling, fighting, and making the reeking air thick with blasphemy. In these dens men and women are indiscriminately mingled; and such men! but more especially, such women! The Enemy of Mankind could not possibly desire more fitting and accomplished instruments to perform all his dirtiest jobs upon earth. Here the striking characteristics of gambling-house, groggery, and brothel are brought in the strongest relief. Whoever glances at one of these places has indelibly stamped upon his brain a picture of human degradation which the most vivid imagination would attempt in vain to conceive. In going about the City, in preparing to discharge a task such as we have undertaken, and exploring the mysteries of these veritable infernal regions, one no longer wonders at the amount and frequency of crime; he only is astonished that it is not a hundred times as great.

We have hinted that the gambling-houses of all grades were well known to the Police: and we now repeat that there is not an officer nor policeman in the City, who doesn't know one or more of these places, and has not in his possession positive evidence of their true character. "Well then, why are they not suppressed, and their keepers punished according to law?" Soft and fair, my good friend! If we could answer that question so that the people could see it exactly as it is, we could revolutionize society, and reform the world. We may say, in general terms, that all these establishments contain or control *votes*—the whole end, aim, and means of office-holders and politicians. There is, doubtless, an immense amount of private bribery of officers by the keepers of these and other unlawful establishments. But the great thing is votes. So long as the party in power can maintain the ascendency by winking at a hundred and fifty notorious gambling-houses, keeping dark about fifteen hundred public brothels, and licensing two thousand superfluous groggeries, so long we shall look in vain for any thorough, radical, and all-embracing system of municipal reform, commended for the benefit of the people, and carried out in complete good faith and honor.

Slice VII.—THE PAWNBROKERS' SHOPS.

We don't know a much more melancholy thing than to ramble through one of the extensive pawnbroking establishments in Chatham-street or the Bowery, crammed with their inconceivable variety of articles of use and luxury, from the broken frying-pan to the diamond necklace. It has seemed to us that it was easy to group the various articles which originally belonged together, and thus make each group tell its own little domestic or personal romance. These pretty half-worn dresses, for example, of a rich material but a long-exploded fashion; and next them this costly but old-fashioned bonnet—this dainty cradle, whose former inmate, if living, must now be grown to man's estate—these rich silver tea-spoons, this bracelet, this massive gold-watch—all these are eloquent memorials of a once happy and prosperous family, driven by some reverse of fortune to poverty and want. The father was a few years ago known as a successful merchant in Front-st., and his family resided in a handsome house up-town, surrounded by every thing to make life a pleasure. But, as he grew more and more prosperous he became also more ambitious, and gradually all the energies of his soul were concentrated in the one consuming desire—to become a *millionaire*. A series of speculations, at first promising, but, as he grew bolder, disastrous, at length left him a ruined man, unless he could raise a large sum of money by a certain day. Every legitimate effort completely failed; and, maddened at the speedy and inevitable destruction of his credit and hopes of fortune, he committed a tremendous forgery—raised the money, saved his credit—and was the next day arrested and thrown into prison as a malefactor. Then came forth the real and inherent cowardice of the man who had possessed courage to sacrifice his honesty and the bread of his wife and family to the demon of Financial Ambition. Secreting a knife from the supper brought by the jailer, he waited till the old prison was sunk in the tomb-like silence of midnight, and then cut his throat. The results of all his mighty scheming lie here. His poor wife and daughters, paralyzed by the fearful blow, found no courage to look their destiny in the face until every thing was swept away from them—home, comfort and all—and their very dresses and household treasures—the cherished cradle where little brother used to sleep—were carried to the pawnbroker's to procure food. Then, when this resource had failed, they had but one way left, that last and dreary hope of destitute and virtuous Woman—the needle. How have they sped? Alas! the poor, pale mother is in the grave, and the two tender daughters are fighting bitterly yet patiently with a bitter world, for bread and shelter. Thus far they have conquered—but when we think how unscrupulous is the tempter with his dazzling promises, and how weak is poor, hungry, unfriended Woman, we tremble for the fate of these poor sisters.

Here is a magnificent diamond necklace, with earrings and bracelet to match—truly a costly and aristocratic casket. They were deposited but a few hours ago, and directly after the following scene had taken place at a fashionable ice-cream saloon in Broadway.—A splendidly-attired woman in the prime of life and loveliness, and bearing unmistakable traces of that easy insolence which marks the "Upper Ten," sits at one of the little marble tables, resting her bonnet (with a bewitching head in it) on her hand and patting her foot rapidly upon the floor. Opposite, and leaning across until his curling hair waves in the fan-breeze she is beckoning into existence, is a gentleman belonging very decidedly to that interesting variety of the species Poodle known as "handsome men."

"My dear madam," the gentleman is going on to say, "if there be any one punishment worse than another, such a horrid monster deserves that it should be inflicted upon him. What, forbid them to credit you at Stewart's!"

"Yes!—and for the paltry amount of $1,500. But my dear Charles, let us speak of your own embarrassments. How much do you want?"

"Generous, noble creature! I intended to have accepted a loan for a thousand—I am morally certain to break the bank with that; but——"

"Enough. Take these jewels—they are worth twice the amount. My husband gave them to me the day before my marriage. I shall manage him well enough."

"Madam! angel of a woman! dearest Clara!"

"Hush, hush! Don't attract attention—good heavens, what are you about, Sir!"

In an hour afterwards "Charles" had spouted the casket and contents for fifteen hundred dollars—the old Shekelite groaning in spirit at the hard bargain the young reprobate drove—and was dining with a plump little actress from the —— Theatre, on woodcock and champagne.

"Ha, ha, ha!" laughed the little witch; "that was nicely done, to be sure. But, Charles, are you *very* sure you don't love this fine goose that lays you so many golden eggs, spoken of in the well-known fable of Esop?"

"Well, I ain't any thing else, girl! But she loves *me* enough for the whole family. She's a trump, though, and here's her health, and fat speculations to her silly old husband."

"Yes—if an old fogy like him will marry a young and dashing wife, why, *caveat emptor!* is my motto."

"There! That infernal red-headed lawyer has been here again! I'll wring his neck one of these days, and send him travelling with his fiery head in his own green bag."

"Oh, ho! Jealous again! Then I'm off. Besides, it is time for me to go and dress. *A revederci!*"

So we will return to the pawnbroker's.

Whom have we here? A very pale, timid-looking little man—thin to diaphony, and with large lustrous eyes that seem like jets welling up from some deep-hidden source. He staggers in under a load of books.

"I want a little money on these books, Sir. They are invaluable to me, and I shall be sure to redeem them as soon as my book is out."

"Don't want books, my good fellow—they don't pay."

"But, Sir, here is Byron, and Shelley, and Bacon, and Jeremy Taylor—"

"Who ish Cheremy Taylor? If it wash Sachary Taylor, now!"

Go away, good scribbler, and lug back your precious books. You will get nothing for them here. The good gentleman who presides over this very respectable establishment has no need of Byron, nor Shelley, nor Bacon, nor Jeremy Taylor. Indeed, it would injure his business if he were to know any thing about them.

But the most interesting part of the pawnbroking business is the stated sales at auction of such articles as have not been redeemed by the owners, and which are put up on the day of sale "in lots to suit purchasers," and generally sold for quite their value. The pawnbroker cares mostly, however, that they bring the amount of his principal and the usurious interest which he is entitled to charge upon his money; for the rest, it is all clear gain. The rate at which he is authorized to charge by law is 25 per cent; but he generally manages by one means or another to double these rates, at least upon the poor laboring people, who constitute a vast majority of his customers. These poor people are frequently compelled to pawn their furniture and their very wearing apparel, to procure bread—hoping that something will turn up to enable them to redeem their property before the time runs out. In this, however, they are too often disappointed, and they go with heavy hearts and tearful eyes to beg a little indulgence from the impassive broker, who, listening very patiently till they tell their story, raises his spectacles to let the glasses cool, and with a shrug and smile that need no cooling, goes on with ciphering up his gains and arranging every thing for the sale. Sometimes a poor widow or orphan comes to plead for some little precious relic of the dead beloved, and will even go down upon her knees before the inexorable penny-turner.—They had better spare their breath to pray for a golden shower to fall upon them from the sky. Such a thing *has* been—but a relenting pawnbroker, never.

On the morning of a regular sale the establishment is thrown open from garret to cellar, to the inspection of such economical housekeepers and professional bargain-hunters as are always on the watch for occasions like this, and whose houses are stored with all sorts of useless trumpery, bought at various times by these notable housewives because it was *so* cheap. Andirons, ambergris, boot-jacks and baby-jumpers, calicoes, cullenders, crimping-irons, cradles, dust-pans and dictionaries, egg-spoons and electrical machines, fiddles and frying-pans, gaiters and go-carts, hampers and hunting-horns, inkstands and ipecac, jewsharps and joint-stools, kaleidescopes, lamps and lavender-water, music, martingals and mattresses, necklaces and nine-pins, optical instruments and oboes, pie-pans and pin-cushions, quack medicines, quills, quicksilver, rings and rat-traps, saddles and shaving-boxes, tongs and tooth-brushes, urns, umbrellas, vandykes and vases, wigs and wicker-baskets, and so on through the alphabet, are crammed together in merciless confusion, looking as if the fragments, thrums, and odds and ends of a dozen communities had been gathered by the chiffoniers and piled into a gigantic rubbish-heap.

The prices obtained at these sales, as we said, are generally fair, and very often even more than the articles are worth—the purchasers supposing that every thing bought at auction must necessarily be cheap. But whatever may be the prices bid at the pawnbroker's sale, the unfortunate owner need expect to receive nothing beyond what may have been originally advanced. The extra interest, costs and charges, commissions, &c. &c., will be pretty sure to eat up any overplus; and the owner, if he demands a settlement, may consider himself very lucky if the pawnbroker don't manage to bring him in debt.

Slice VIII.—THE MOCK AUCTIONS.

We hope our country acquaintance, Mr. Greenhorn, will excuse us when we tell him we don't sympathize much with his loss in buying a splendid gold watch for fifteen dollars, and a casket of diamonds for eighteen-pence a piece. If he supposed (as he protests) that they were genuine, he must have known that they were stolen, to be sold at any such price; and he has allowed his appetite for a sharp bargain to get the upper hand of his honesty as well as his usual shrewdness. We tell him plainly, then, that his intention was to avail himself of somebody's being robbed. If he has got bitten, who is to pity him?

Notwithstanding that we don't sympathize with Mr. Greenhorn, we condemn the villany of Mr. Funk, as roundly as the roundest. He is infinitely less respectable than the burglar or the blackleg, and deserves a severer punishment. There are rascalities enough, Heaven knows, in trade, in the best of streets, and under the most virtuous auspices. From the heavy importer of Water-street to the three-penny retailer on the corner, lies are told every day enough to place anybody who *had* a soul in extreme jeopardy. But the Peter Funk is the sublime of mercantile swindling—the result of the commercial principle carried to its ultimates. The thing he does upon a scale of magnificent falsehood and impudence, is done by the dealer in diluted brandies and damaged calicoes upon a smaller scale, in a more sneaking manner. Mr. Funk sells our friend Greenhorn a pinchbeck watch for gold, and real glass beads set in pewter for diamonds. Well—what then? The respectable house of Wiggins & Winkle sells us, yes *us*, the veritable writer of these "Slices," a catty-box of real Souchong, into which has been mixed ten or a dozen pounds of Bohea, and a basket of champagne which they know to be galvanized cider, and which cost them ten cents a gallon. Our wife buys a new frock at Blinkum's, which she is assured is the real French chintz, warranted fast colors, and which, after the first washing, looks like the fag-end of a consumptive rainbow. In fact, he or she who *buys* any thing anywhere, must keep a sharp look-out. Let a person take a thousand dollars and start down Broadway, buying at every shop and paying whatever is asked, without question or hesitation, and how much do you think his purchases would be actually worth by the time his money gave out? And yet, the shopkeepers are honest and respectable—have pews in church, and have two gowns, and every thing tidy and comfortable.

Peter Funk is a gentleman of extensive connections, and has establishments in various parts of the city besides Chatham street and Lower Broadway. You may find the red flag of Peter Funkism flying in Pearl-street and other "heavy" quarters, where it is generally supposed that transactions are *bona fide* and dealers responsible. There are pinchbeck and glass beads in many other kinds of goods besides watches and breastpins. The country merchant, who buys from a sample, and takes the "invoice" measurement, (forged in the back office,) is frequently amazed upon opening his bales, to discover that he has bought a pig in the poke—that his splendid English prints have become metamorphosed into cheap domestics, and that his woad-dyed French broadcloth smells horribly of logwood. In truth, the whole auction system, although there are of course individual exceptions, is false and hollow, conducted upon a wrong basis, and depending for its profits upon the shrewdness of those who sell and the gullibility of those who buy.

The organization of the mock auctions is complete, and each shop is the centre of a conspiracy against the pockets of the community, requiring six or eight accomplices to carry on business successfully. Besides the auctioneer and his clerk there are the outsiders, who always attend the sale and bid on every thing that is offered—making bargains by the score, each one of which, according to their own story, ought to enrich them. Men are employed by the day to stand outside the counter to act as false bidders. We have seen men in the mock-auction rooms in Broadway within the last few days, whom we have known to be engaged in the same business for ten years. They are generally men of middle age and of honest looks. Then there is the "respectable jeweller" round the corner or across the way, to whom the doubtful or hesitating are referred as to the genuineness of the article for sale, and who is always ready to give a favorable answer. This is done, too, very safely; for in the case of a gold watch, for instance, the Peter Funk, whom Mr. Greenhorn takes to be a rival bidder, takes you to the jeweller and exhibits a *real* gold watch for his inspection. The verdict is of course favorable; and, on the way back, the watches are dexterously exchanged in the outside pocket of the Funk, and you go on bidding for what you now suppose you *know* to be a genuine lever, Tobias make, full jewelled. So with the articles of jewelry—pencils, rings, breastpins, necklaces, &c. &c. The whole arrangement is perfect, and such an air of earnestness and sincerity is preserved by the accomplices on the outside of the counter, that an inexperienced stranger cannot fail to be taken in.

But the peculiar feature of this business is, that the poor dupe never knows *how many* articles he is buying. For instance, the auctioneer holds up a card containing a dozen or two of small articles, and asks, "How much a-piece, gentlemen, for these splendid gold pencil-cases, very heavy, and warranted eighteen carats. The last of an immense stock from a Broadway establishment, just become bankrupt, and sold under the orders of the Sheriff. How much for these magnificent pencils, breastpins, and bracelets?" The Funks make a small bid, which he receives with virtuous indignation, and perhaps ventures to inquire whether they think the articles were stolen. Upon this another Funk bids a higher sum, and the greenhorn begins to think that here is indeed a chance for a splendid bargain. At length he bids, and his fate is sealed. After playing him a little, as Frank Forrester would play a trout, down goes the hammer, and the fortunate purchaser, who supposes he has bid off two dozen articles, is taken into the back room to settle and receive his goods. Here an immense box of all sorts of trash, from a pair of scissors to a shirt-button, is produced, and he learns, to his consternation, that he has purchased seven or eight hundred pieces at twenty-five cents a piece; and a bill for a couple of hundred dollars is presented to him. If he remonstrates, the clerk is inflexible; and if he attempts to leave the place, he is forcibly withheld—a Funk is called in, who passes himself off for an officer, and he is threatened with immediate arrest for "obtaining goods under false pretences." Alarmed and dumbfounded, he pays over all the money he has about him, and is kindly permitted to take his purchase—leaving his watch in pledge that he will return and settle the balance of the bill. With his load of rubbish tied up in his pocket-handkerchief, he makes his escape; and, entering the first jeweller's shop he encounters, is politely told, with a well-bred shrug of pity, that his whole cargo isn't worth five dollars. But then the lesson he has learned, if he only knows how to profit by it, will stand him well in stead for the money he has thrown away.

Let all strangers remember, once for all, that there is no establishment in the city where real watches and valuable jewelry are sold at auction. Such goods have always a nearly fixed and intrinsic value; and can neither be bought nor sold at any great reduction from the standard price. Whoever offers them thus is a swindler or a thief. Either he has stolen what he sells, or else the articles he offers are nothing but paste and galvanized pewter, and are utterly worthless. By following this plain direction, the stranger in New York will save his money and avoid being obliged to regard himself as a fool and a spooney.

If anybody would like to know why these shops are not suppressed by law, he must ask the "proper authorities"—if he can find them. It is none of our business. We expose the various devices which exist openly in the Metropolis, whose express and only business it is to defraud the unwary. If the authorities, who are perfectly cognizant of their existence, would do as much to suppress them, the evil would soon be abated.

We hope, while on this subject, we shall be pardoned for a few profitable speculations—things not often made by editors of newspapers. While passing these mock-auction establishments, and wondering for the hundred-thousandth time at the gullibility of human nature, we have sometimes asked ourselves what would be the result if all the mock auctions in the community were at once to be exposed? The sleek-fed proselytist with his mock religion; the virtuous lady leaving her splendid mansion "above Bleecker" to meet her paramour in Church-street; the respectable merchant or professional man spending his time and his income at the gambling-house or the brothel; the demagogue dealing out his pernicious slang and mock patriotism to gaping fools; the mercenary editor selling his columns to the interest or the institution that would pay him best; the financier originating falsehoods to facilitate his extensive operations and swell his profits; the painted harlot making merchandise of her mock blushes and impoisoned charms; the lawyer selling his genius and learning to well-fed oppression—would it not be a sight worth seeing? and after contemplating it should we not be ready to exclaim, "The whole world is but one vast Mock Auction!"

Slice IX.—THE INTELLIGENCE OFFICES.

You have often, reader, as you have ridden by in an omnibus, or hurried along on foot, given a glance at the Intelligence Offices, crowded like a female mass-meeting, with women in outlandish, hot-looking dresses, as if they had been originally made for somebody else, and worn most perseveringly out of season. If in the midst of Summer, with the sweltering air full of fiery dust, and the sidewalk blistering your feet through your boot-soles, an intolerable glare of crimson and scarlet shawls, ribands, and faded bonnet-flowers, with a sultry sense of yellow calico past all endurance, is sure to issue from one of these places and stream clear across the street. Perhaps you may have wondered, for a moment, what was going on inside these dark and suffocating places, and hazarded a speculation as to who and what were all the women packed in there so closely.

But in New York we have not much time for looking after what does not concern us, and still less for thinking about it. If you were to enter one of these dens where "intelligence" is peddled at half a dollar a dose, you would be struck with the diversity yet similarity of faces congregated there. Anxiety blended with stolidity, hope and disappointment, sagacity and uncouthness—these go to make up the face of the female immigrant. The unnatural and degrading position she occupies—forced to beg and even pay for the chance of being selected for somebody's domestic slave—sent all over the City, often on a fool's errand, and often to endure the vulgar insolence of some sister woman who happens to have a house and a husband, only to be told at last, in grating and harsh terms, that "she won't do," or her "references are not satisfactory," or "I don't like your looks," and to go back desponding and heart-broken to resume her seat on the pine bench of the Intelligence Office, until some other Mrs. Arrogance sends for a servant—such, day after day, is the fate of the poor immigrant girl. Who can wonder that she thus in time becomes hardened and indifferent, and that when at last she does get a place, and finds herself treated and spoken to rather as a dog than a human being, her stock of patience and endurance gives out, and she determines to repay brutality with audacity, degradation with ill-humor, and oppression with hypocrisy? We hear loud complaints on all hands of the unfaithfulness and idleness of servants; but we have never yet known a woman who treated those under her management like human beings, having hearts and affections, and aspirations and sensibilities, who was ever robbed by her servants, deceived by them, or her household or children neglected. On the contrary, a little common humanity shown these poor, homeless, friendless creatures—a very little—rouses at once the strongest and most uncontrollable sentiment in the female heart—gratitude—and they love you and all that belongs to you with a deep and self-sacrificing affection. If we but knew how far a little kindness and good-heartedness goes in alleviating the unhappiness of the children of want and poverty, we might all be at least rich in our charities!

If you step in from the street—or rather down, for it is quite likely that we are going down cellar to pursue our investigations—you will see perched up behind a sort of desk or magisterial tribune, a small, bald-headed man with piercing black eyes, large, flabby under lip and sixty years, who appears to be poring constantly over a thin, dog-eared memorandum-book, something of the form and general appearance of the "ledger" at a grocery and provision store on any corner. If you look more closely, however, you will perceive that the little man is every now and then gloating over his female congregation with the eye of a *dilettante* satyr, letting his glance fall for a moment here and there as it encounters some unusually young and wholesome face or some swelling and elastic form.

But here comes a customer—a portly and comely-looking matron, who has driven up in her carriage—(you can see it is not a cab, for the driver, although it is melting midsummer, wears a long drab-cloth surtout buttoned tightly to his chin and the shoulders covered with six capes.) The lady herself is highly rouged and white-balled, and over-dressed to decided vulgarity.—But that is nothing—we have seen quite as stylish a turn-out in the front sofas of the Astor-place Opera, and there is no doubt that our customer belongs to the Upper Ten Thousand—as we shall probably ascertain by listening to their conversation. The keeper of the den bows low as she sails up to his desk, although a twinkle and a leer in his malicious eyes belie this testimonial of respect. The lady speaks:

"Have you any help you can recommend to-day, Teddy?"

"Yes, madam, I have a couple of delicate craythers there, just come over. But they are both Catholics, and you know how obstinate they are."

"Never mind. Send them round this afternoon—No. — ——-st. you know. Mind and impress them with the idea that they must look well to their references. I'm very particular, you know. Which are they?"

"Them in the corner there. Catharine and Jinny, come here, my darlings. Ye're in luck to-day. Here's a lady who will take both of you on trial, and if ye can bring good characthers, and suit her well, ye may have easy work and good pay as long as iver ye like."

"Yes—I want two steady, faithful, trustworthy girls—and for such I am willing to pay the very highest wages. Call at five this afternoon and bring your references."

Is it necessary to trace this infamous transaction any farther in detail? Eager to procure work, and delighted at the chance thus offered, the unsuspecting girls go to the house designated, which we need not say is a place of assignation and prostitution, kept by the fine lady with the carriage. Here, after a proper preparation, during which they are bewildered and excited by the glowing promises and prospects held out by their eloquent mistress, they are introduced to two respectable elderly gentlemen—one a rich stock-broker from Wall-street, and the other a heavy importer in South-street,—both of course pillars of Society, exemplary husbands and fathers, and whose morality is as untarnished as their credit. If the poor girls, however, hesitate and struggle for their virtue—the only thing left them in the wide, dreary world—a little elixir of a peculiar nature creates a temporary insanity, during which their ruin is completed, and they are made fiends against their will—sent out as ministers of death to make awful war upon that sex by whom they fell. But they must be careful! If they should happen to be caught in a row, or with a gentleman's purse in their fingers, they will be punished with all the rigor of the law. But the respectable stock-broker and heavy importer, will they not be punished? Oh no—quite the contrary. They are ornaments of society, and are supposed to have made a hundred thousand dollars a-piece by the last steamer! And the woman, the mistress of this horrible place, what will they do with her? Oh nothing. She pays her rent regularly, and has money in the bank. The magistrates, too, are her friends, and she could tell a great many disagreeable secrets, if she were to be offended. It is the poor girls alone who suffer.

Wise City Fathers! We tell you plainly that many of these "intelligence offices" are moral "fences," a thousand times more dangerous, more pestiferous to Society, than all the ship-fever ever imported, and destroying by hundreds the souls and bodies of honest and innocent young women whose only desire is for work and bread, and who are lured into these infernal dens by the lying promises of their inhuman keepers. Look to it, and see if you can discover any of these hidden causes of the deep, damning, and wide-spread licentiousness that is converting your beautiful City into a moral hell—a Gomorrah, deserving only to be consumed by the fire of Heaven.

The ostensible business of many intelligence offices is mostly sham or imposition. The keepers generally do nothing for either employer or employed until they have been feed; and when the silver is fingered their interest in the matter, either way, ceases. Nine-tenths of the indescribable trouble, the disaster, the agony, of housekeeping, in New York, which constitute such constant themes of eloquent lamentation whenever two or three housekeepers meet, arise from the loose, dishonest Intelligence Office system. No careful housewife will ever apply a second time at an Intelligence Office for a servant. One lesson respecting the manner in which they fulfil the large and ample promises of their advertisements is quite sufficient! If you leave a request for a first-rate cook, you are likely to be sent a raw girl who has never in her life got farther in the culinary art than boiling potatoes with their jackets on, and who is as profoundly ignorant of the mysteries of cooking a beef-steak as the editor of the —— —— is of truth or decency.

And so of every thing else. You might as well expect to get the truth out of a politician, or charity from a millionaire, as to procure what you are promised at an Intelligence Office.

We do not mean to say that there is not, here and there, an exception to our remarks, nor have we the slightest intention of designating individuals —that is the duty of the authorities, not of the press.—Our only purpose is to characterize and expose the *system*. In a City like New York—the headquarters of an immigration that comes pouring from an old world to the new one by hundreds of thousands per annum—some better method of finding and distributing employment to the throngs of strangers should be adopted than the present inefficient and demoralizing one. Since it is neither possible nor desirable to arrest the course of immigration, our authorities ought at least to recognise officially this immense movement, and to provide against as many of its evils as possible. A little investigation would enable them to do great good and to prevent gigantic evils and oppressions, by adopting some simple and efficient mode of making honest employers and seekers for work acquainted with each other. We build costly custom-houses and employ hundreds of well-fed clerks to see that our importations of goods are all properly conducted—while we leave our immense importations of human beings to fall a prey to every species of villain who chooses to pounce upon them.

Slice X.—THE MARKETS.

Most of our readers have doubtless had "slices" from the Markets before now. But they furnish abundant mental food as well as physical, to one who has learned the grand secret of eating with his eyes. We scarcely know where so much and such varieties of human nature can be encountered as in a walk through the Markets. Every face you meet is a character, every scene affords a piquant contrast. Talk of your Eastern bazaars and Parisian arcades! of your white-footed oriental gazelle and your brown-cheeked, mischief-colored grisette—your kirtled Albanian—by the way, will any man of veracity tell us what *is* a kirtle ?—and your kilted Highlander! Why, they are the merest common-place people, place them side by side with the butcher-boy of the market; the old huckster-woman who implores you in all weathers to buy her vegetables, although she has a handsome house at home and fifty thousand dollars out at interest, (we hope not in the Moonshine Insurance Company,)—the pretty, bare-armed girl who comes to buy breakfast for the mistress and must av coorse have the best of every thing—the modest mechanic's wife, who surveys the aristocratic turkey and the lordly sirloin with a sigh, and then, with a timid glance at the little stock of change, is fain to put up with a lean joint for dear John's dinner. But then it will be cooked by her own fair hands, and she herself will shell the peas and boil the potatoes and dress the baby ; and if the mutton itself *is* a little tough, her glance of love as her husband enters the door, will be so tender, and will speak a heart so true, that handsome John will not miss the stall-fed luxury that his earnings would not procure, while he owns so much hearty happiness which wealth could not buy and the world cannot take away. Whew! what a sentence!

Then here is the dainty cit, his boots so nicely black, and his shirt-bosom so unimpeachably white. He knows the nicest tit-bits and the tenderest points in a steak or a roaster at a glance. He has almost an instinct in the selection of asparagus, and the cauliflowers he buys looks as if they were raised for him on purpose, in a special garden. Yonder rushes the Hotel-keeper, fearful that somebody has brought something to market which he shall not see. He has but one ungratified wish; if he could buy *every thing* in market of a morning and then select a dinner at leisure! What a bill of fare he would have; and how he would invite the Editors to dine with him, and how he would get puffed in all the newspapers!

Yonder comes creeping faintly along a thin, meager, sick old lady, meanly clad, and haggard from care and anxiety. She carries with difficulty a basket on her arm, in which she has already got a scraggy quarter of dark brown veal, a half-peck of peas, yellow as old maidenhood and hard as bullets—and two bunches of asparagus, looking like a pair of Irish bogs in miniature. She is now bargaining for some musty dried apples, which will be in due time converted into pies for the people. That—could you mistake her for a moment?—that is the Private Boarding-house Keeper. She rents a large house in Dash-st., which is described in her advertisement in the *Daily Tribune*, as containing "genteel furnished apartments in a fashionable neighborhood." The parlor has a faded Brussels carpet, patched with in-grain; half a dozen mahogany chair skeletons, a broken lounge, a rickety armchair with a piece of cotton netting spread carefully over the top, two ottomans as immutable as milestones from a defect in the underpinnings, and a piano of the time of Louis le Grand—although it is by no means a grand piano. She here "takes in" young lawyers, dentists without extraction, sub-editors, and shopkeepers just started in business, with a hired counter and show-window in Grand-street.

The Markets of New York are justly celebrated for the plenty and variety with which they are supplied at all seasons—the demands of the great metropolis bringing here producers of all sorts from a long distance, attracted by the brisk demand and high prices invariably created by the presence of any really good or superior article. In fresh Butter and Vegetables even the western portion of New Jersey and the vicinity of Philadelphia itself are constant and large contributors. The west bank of the Delaware is said to have been planted, near Philadelphia, by the Swedes, (who were the early settlers,) with a peculiar kind of grass, that imparts a rich and luscious flavor to the Butter produced there, which cannot be equalled elsewhere. Thus the shrewd Huckster, when butter in Philadelphia is worth but 23 or 25 cents per pound, buys up the choicest lots in that market and sends them to New York, where they are sure of a ready sale at almost any price that may be demanded. So with Berries and Fruits. The earliest Strawberries and the finest Peaches pass by Philadelphia and are sold in the New York market. In Poultry the Philadelphia trade is very extensive and lucrative.

The Fish Markets are a very interesting feature of the New York Market

System. No other point in the Union offers so great a variety of excellent Fish, from all longitudes and latitudes, and always at the earliest moment at which they are accessible. From the plump and rosy Salmon of Portland to the piquant Pompion of Pensacola and the Green Turtle of the Keys, every species of substantial and rare Fish can be found in the Markets of New York. The Green Lobster destined to be parboiled till he changes his politics, the spicy Shad, the noble Halibut and Rock, the Catfish, the Perch, the Sea and Striped Bass, the fresh Mackerel and Cod, are always here in their season, and offered to the public in a cleanly and satisfactory manner. Indeed, Fish and Fishing, of all sorts, are carried on in New York upon the most extensive *scale.*

The Meat Markets occupy the principal places in our Markets, and the stalls, being rented to private individuals, are kept emulously clean and wholesome. The Butchers are generally obliging and attentive; although our duty compels us to say that many rumors are afloat of distillery beef, premature death, &c. &c., which it gives us a qualm in the stomach merely to think of. It is the best way, in all such cases, to believe as little as possible of what you hear—and therefore we believe nothing. The Butchers form a powerful and respectable body of citizens, and are thoroughly organized into a Mutual Benefit Association, which regulates prices and enforces its rules strictly. There are between six and seven hundred regular Butchers in the City; and probably fewer unworthy members in the trade than in any other calling. They are among our most quiet and amiable citizens, and are in no wise responsible for the goings-on of the "Butcher-boys," with whom they are often ignorantly confounded. Their trade is a thrifty and appears to be a wholesome one. Such a thing as a lean Butcher, or a Butcher in want, has never been heard of.

The Poultry, Vegetable, Fruit, Butter, Cheese, and Egg Markets are all jumbled up together in most admired disorder, and are generally carried on by hucksters, who forestall the market by buying up large quantities of fresh articles, when they are low, and keeping them until a rise, when of course they are stale and unwholesome. This is the greatest evil connected with our Market System, and one which it is very surprising has not long ago been broken up. Very few producers come face to face with the consumers of their merchandise; the Hucksters snapping up every thing valuable, and then "taking their time" to turn it to the best advantage. In this way, the citizens pay from fifteen to fifty *per cent.* more than is received by the producer, besides being almost invariably served with a stale article. The immense Fruit and Berry trade, the Egg-trade, Butter, Cheese, &c., are the most subject to the Huckstering System. It is an application, in a small way, of the evils and costliness of the "Mercantile System," and is a serious and constant drain upon the purse as well as punishment to the palate, and even to health itself. It is not likely that it will ever be put down—but nobody can help wishing that it might be.

On the whole, the Markets in New York, in their extent, conduct, and accommodations, are by no means equal to the wants or reputation of the City. A great and thorough movement on this subject will some day be started and carried out, which will give New York a Market, constructed upon modern principles, combining taste with utility, and adding to the City what will be one of its greatest ornaments as well as blessings.

A plan has always found favor with us—and has been several times alluded to in *The Tribune*—for creating a spacious and substantial market through the whole extent of Canal-st., cutting that splendid avenue through to the East River, at its present width. This would be the most magnificent market in the world—central and convenient for all classes. The advantages of a great central market running transversely across the Island will too readily suggest themselves to require being more than alluded to. New York in ten years from this day will be the first city of the world—if not absolutely in population, yet in enterprise, taste, wealth, splendor, and public spirit. Within that time the whole upper part of the Island will be incrusted with beautiful palaces and exquisite cottage residences, starting out or hiding modestly, like the fairy pictures one sees in dreams; while the vast mart of trade, commerce, literature, and omnibuses, will have crept gradually up Broadway and along either river, until our projected Canal-st. Market, stretched from the East River to the Hudson, would find itself in the centre of business and down-town.

When these things come to pass—as they surely will—New York will be such a city as the modern world has never seen, and will even then have but commenced upon its vigorous and promising childhood. Of its mature manhood who shall speak?

Slice XI.—THE B'HOYS.

A STRANGER might live a lifetime in New York without forming acquaintance with this extraordinary class of beings, or even seeing them, except in case of a general conflagration, or on their way to a target-shooting excursion, or a musical festival at Biddle's Grove, or a flotilla ball, or a torchlight procession, or some such peculiarly New Yorkish turn-out. And yet one cannot be said to really know New-York—to understand in what way its human nature is different from other human nature—without studying the habits and character of the B'hoys. It is true that we have recently had a representation upon the stage of a pretended type of this extraordinary development of the social animal—and presented, too, in a likeness which all seemed readily enough to recognise. But yet the portrait was a false one, and gave only the more conspicuous deformities of the character. Indeed, a mirror so foul and distorted as the modern stage could not be expected to reflect any thing but the obvious faults, vices, and barbarisms of whomsoever was brought before it; and therefore it is that, while the B'hoy himself possesses many of the noble and truly manly attributes which go a-begging in genteel society, our Mose and Jakey and Sykesey of the stage are nothing more nor better than absolute and unmitigated ruffians, whom to do any thing but loathe, would be in itself a sin.—The B'hoy, as we see him on the stage, is only in his out-door, midnight, rowdy aspect; and it is a lamentable thing enough that instead of endeavoring to elevate the character and stimulate the ambition of the spectators, by showing them one of themselves in his better phase, the getters-up of these execrable representations should have gained a temporary popularity by bringing out only the coarser and more vulgar traits, and thus enlisting the brutal sympathies and passions of their audiences. Many a half-timid young man, struggling between the dictates of his better nature and the promptings of a depraved appetite, has been confirmed in vicious courses by witnessing and contributing to the applauses with which the beastly exuberance of "Mose" was received from the stage.

It is in his domestic character and associations that the B'hoy commands most of our respect. Many of the roughest and most untamable specimens of these beings—who are first at a fray and ever ready for a feast or a frolic, a knock-down-and-drag-out—practise the social virtues with a sincerity and to an extent rare enough among classes of far higher pretensions and opportunities. Thrown into the world in childhood without guide or protector, and with no means of education, or worse still, no one to inspire in them the desire for education, they grow up like wild weeds and must inevitably produce bitter and unwholesome fruit. And yet, in despite of this utter lack of culture and development, many of them become tender husbands, and, like other wild animals, seem to reserve all the nobleness and susceptibility of their natures to lavish it upon their mates and offspring, while to all the rest of creation they show nothing but teeth and claws.—Another virtue which they possess in a high degree is friendship. Full of rough play, and uncouthly sociable as a company of young bears—often even quarrelling and fighting among themselves—yet let an enemy appear, or let a friend be threatened with danger, and they are devotion itself, freely risking life and limb in defence of a companion, and sharing with him when unfortunate their home and purse, homely and scanty though they may be, with a natural and cordial hospitality which is the consecrated poetry of poverty. They are brave, easily led astray, but not naturally wicked. They are good, unselfish, frolicsome creatures, whose misfortune is that a rude contact with society, under unfavorable auspices, has served to ripen and bring out only a certain class of functions and attributes, while the intellectual and moral faculties which could alone have given them value or useful direction, have been repressed and stunted. Thus, their courage is quarrelsomeness; their frankness is vulgarity; their magnanimity subsides to thriftlessness; their fun expands to rowdyism; their feeling of friendship and brotherhood seeks dangerous activity in mobs and gangs who conspire against the public peace.

The worst feature in the character of the B'hoy is his dissipation—his worst enemy the grog-shop, the three-cent cellar, or the liquor-grocery on the corner. Deprived by position and finally by inclination of respectable associations—and especially of the refining influence of cultivated female society—his restrained social instinct, his ambition, his desire to struggle and shine, which he shares in common with all man and woman kind, lead him to the rum-shop and to the haunts of the vicious and the vile. Here he finds himself, from the audacity of his temper and the strength of his arm, an object of consideration and regard. His vanity is flattered and his appetites awakened, until he gladly embraces the career of vulgar rowdyism—simply because he must have *some* career, and there is no other within his reach. The writer of this sketch has been with the B'hoys, at many times and in many circumstances, determined to learn all that could be learned by study and observation respecting a class of mankind so peculiar and so interesting; and he does not hesitate to record his testimony in favor of the goodness of their natures and the nobleness of their original capacities, while at the same time he admits and deplores the degradation into which most of them have fallen. Many of the coolest as well as most daring acts of courage during the late Mexican war were performed by these men, while at the same time their character for subordination, modesty, and temperance was unimpeachable. Now war is at best but a coarse, low master, and not much calculated to add dignity or refinement to the human character. But it teaches discipline, obedience, and punctuality, and discountenances bluster and disorder; and even this was enough to greatly change the B'hoy from bad to better, and to show clearly of what, under still more favorable circumstances, he would be capable. Suppose, for instance, Government should take into its head one of these days to organize an army of Volunteer Agriculturists, under General Skinner, and an efficient *corps* of officers from the American Institute instead of West Point—armed with hoes, rakes, scythes, and cradles, artilleried with ploughs and harrows, and furnished forth with a complement of cattle, seeds, and all necessary utensils, and ordered to the frontier to conquer a piece from the wilderness instead of the Mexicans—and suppose that every soldier in this grand army were permitted to take his wife and children, or his sweetheart, and were given in fee simple a nice little farm, sufficient for all the wants of himself and family—what a glorious chance would this be for the B'hoy! and how much less national money and national crime it would cost, and how much happiness instead of death and mourning it would entail! As soon as civilization arrives at years of discretion, and is able to see what ails it, we expect to see, in some such way as this, our cities purged of rowdyism, and the incentives to theft, robbery, and prostitution greatly abated, while at the same time clear swing and ample reward will be granted to Labor and Intelligence, and the coffers of the nation enriched by the creation of new and prosperous communities, replenishing the granaries whence Europe must draw her sustenance, and consuming immense amounts of our own manufactures.

But the B'hoy thinks little of his future destiny, and seems unconscious of any higher powers than those brought into play by a race for a fire-plug or a scamper on the avenue. His strongest passion seems fun, and to its gratification even his rowdyism is made subservient. He revels in a spirit of broad, coarse humor, sparing nothing in its way, and finding its delight in hard knocks as well as droll conceits. A fight is a capital joke, and a crown is cracked as though it might be a conundrum. Even in the worst of times, when spanners and brickbats fly thick as hail, and the blood of No. 42 is up so high that it escapes at the nose, there is as much fun as ferocity, and the affair is regarded rather as a frolic than a riot. It is true that such rough-and-tumble business might be considered by our dainty bloods in Broadway as somewhat too serious for a joke; but the B'hoys don't mean any harm by it. A good strong "muss" is the only safety-valve through which can escape their immense exuberance of animal spirits.

If you would see the B'hoy, however, in his glory—at the top of his career—in the *ne plus ultra* of his mundane state—you must see him taking a drive with his G'hal on the avenues. Get out of the way, common people, and stand aside, slow nags, till the elephant passes. Whoorah! here he comes, shouting and singing with a sort of Titanic jollity, like Cyclops on a bender, and calling with whip and voice upon his "crab" to "go it or break a leg!"—while LIZE, clinging to the seat with a death-grip in either hand, lowers her Bowery cut-water so as to present the smallest possible space to the atmosphere, and setting her teeth hard and bracing her feet firmly against the foot-board, is prepared for any emergency. Here everybody is on an equality, save that whoever has the fastest horse is the best

man. The aristocratic dandy of the Opera, the spendthrift clerk from Front-street, the flashy sporting-man with his unimpeachable turn-out, all go the same road and appear upon the same level. Social inequalities are, like the avenue itself, Macadamized—though much more evenly, unless it has mended its ways since last we rode over its dusty billows until we got thoroughly sea-sick. Of a fine afternoon it swarms with veritable specimens of the B'hoy, arrayed in outre vest and funnel-legged panties, and with an enormous crape band around the hat, on their way to Cato's, or the Red House, or Stryker's Bay, or the High Bridge, or some other of the innumerable resorts of out-of-town visitants, with which the vicinity of New York is planted.

Another scene dear to the tender sensibilities of the B'hoy is the prize-fight—that most brutal exhibition of a degraded and bestialized humanity. Here the influence of the scene adds ferocity to every evil propensity and sharpens depraved appetite with the scent of blood.—The influence of a prize-fight upon minds and characters thus prepared to receive its horrid teachings cannot be otherwise than fatal. The young rowdy, still retaining some faint glimmerings of that refinement which Nature bestows even upon her humblest children, will, on his first visit to a prize-fight, have all the good completely obliterated, and all the evil strengthened and confirmed. The fierce excitement of human battle—the blood, the bravoes, the ambition, the dauntless courage and contempt for pain and danger, and even life, which make up the elements of a prize-fight, leave their impress indelibly upon heart and brain, and are of themselves enough to stamp with heaven-defacing brutality the lineaments of the human soul that takes delight in them. From the prize-fighter's ring emanates that bloody and bull-dog spirit which fills our streets with ruffians and disgraces civilization and the age with scenes and incidents worthy only of the savage in his wilderness. And yet, these bloody outrages upon public decency and morality—these cattle-shows and premium fairs of human demonism—are permitted to be advertised week after week in some of the public papers, and to take place in the very suburbs of the metropolis, without any efficient step being taken by the authorities to put a stop to them. Not many years ago a young man was actually beaten to death in the ring and breathed his last in the arms of his bottle-holder. It made quite a noise at the time, and we remember that the groggeries and tiger dens in Park-place and Centre-street and Chatham-street and the Sixth Ward generally were in quite a flutter for several hours. But they had no need. The papers stormed a little, the Police Office blustered a little, and that was all. In a few months after, a company of two or three hundred rowdies, having bragged of what they were about to do for weeks beforehand, embarked at midnight on the East River and crossed over to Connecticut, where the champions, surrounded by their partisans and friends, battered and bruised each other for six or eight hours and returned to the City unmolested—with the exception of a trifling interruption by a Connecticut deacon, who soon got his spectacles smashed and was driven off the premises with a black eye and a flea in his ear.

Now there is no use, we suppose, of blowing up the authorities for not doing their plain and manifest duty in suppressing with the strong hand these and similar public wrongs; but it appears certain that if they *would* bestir themselves and put down these prize-fights and fire-riots, and abolish three-quarters of the groggeries and other vile haunts of rowdyism, the moral atmosphere would at once become purified, and the B'hoy—whom we are now compelled to regard as the disgrace of the times—would become a cheerful, industrious, well-to-do, and valuable member of the community.—But for all these desirable meliorations we must wait the slow yet inevitable movement which civilization, amid many struggles and backslidings, is yet ever making in an onward and upward direction.

Slice XII.—THE FIREMEN.

It is a very common, almost universal mistake, to suppose that the word Fireman is synonymous with "rowdy." Because there are a few hundred of lawless boys and lazy "fancy-men," supported by their mistresses, who hang about the midnight oyster-cellars and three-cent groggeries, and start at the first stroke of the fire-bell, or get up false alarms on purpose to have a "muss"—or hang round the engine-houses, fighting and quarrelling with each other, and waylaying respectable females obliged to be out after dark—every one takes it for granted that the great body of Firemen are of a similar kidney. It is surprising to us that this extensive and pervading error has not long before now been set right, and the public informed of that which is really the case—that the vast majority of the Firemen—those who really do the hard work and expose themselves to incredible hardships and dangers, without pay or any reward save the approval of their own consciences, in defending the lives and property of the community—are in fact worthy, hard-working citizens, and condemn with all their hearts the doings of their reputed associates, which have so disgraced the City, and cast odium upon a noble and heroic class of men. We have made ourselves intimately acquainted, from personal observation, with the general character of our Firemen; and we unhesitatingly pronounce them, in the main, as orderly, virtuous, and well-behaved a class of men as we have in the community. They regret, as much as any man can do, the character and conduct of the rowdy gangs of discharged butcher-boys and underbred blacklegs who assume the red shirt of the Fireman in which to bully and bluster in safety, and whose highest ambition appears to be to live without work, and "run with the engine."

These loafers are, for the most part, the "fancy-men" of certain Cyprians, who receive their visits one day in the week, and supply them with money from their own infamous and abhorrent traffic.

These "lovyers," receiving thus from their mistresses a little money, live at the butter-cake shops and lie basking in the sun or loafing at the corners during the day. But, as soon as night comes on, they enter upon a new life. . The holes and corners of the City are ransacked in search of adventures—some lie in ambuscade in the squares or remote quarters of the City, to pounce upon and rob unsuspecting passengers, or to insult, and often to outrage, in the most fiendish manner, such women as may pass. They are generally too cunning to become thieves, and refuse to run the risk of the State Prison for any thing less than a rape or a promising robbery. Nine-tenths of these villains are red-hot politicians, and it is they who assist to swell the almost incredible majorities in certain well-known wards and districts—majorities which serve to keep the City Government for the most part in wrong hands, and to prevent the suppression of the glaring evils we have been delineating in these Numbers, by the unsparing and honest execution of the laws.

We doubt if a more desperate and reckless set of rascals could be gathered together in the purlieus of St. Giles or the *Cité*, than those that infest New York. Prowling about the darkest and filthiest quarters of the City, carousing with the abandoned Five Pointesses at the groceries on the corners, gathering at the gambling-house, spreading themselves over the town in search of desperate adventures, they form a regular *cordon* of rascality, through which it is worth a woman's honor or a man's life to penetrate. They are well known to the police, and commit wickedness enough every week to send them to the State Prison or the Penitentiary. Why, then, are they not arrested and their gangs broken up? Sage inquirer! You must have recently arrived from the country, or you would not have asked that question. These fellows can all vote, ay, not merely once, but twice or thrice, if necessary; and they can also take possession of a poll and hold it all day—permitting none but their own friends to approach.

But the real Firemen, who do the hard work and say nothing about it, are a very different set of men. For the most part engaged in honest callings—many of them being journeymen mechanics, some clerks or assistants in respectable establishments, or often master mechanics and proprietors—they are ever ready, in a quiet, prompt way, to don the fire-cap and put their hands and shoulders to the work of saving their neighbor's property—constantly performing feats of courage and daring that would make a hero of the battle-field hesitate, and exposing themselves to the most imminent peril, with a coolness that a knight of the crusades might envy. We hope our readers have not forgotten the incident at the commencement of the great fire of 1845, when the store of Crocker & Warren exploded with saltpetre, (*will* saltpetre explode?) and blew the roof, upon which were two Firemen, entirely over another building, depositing it on the ground at some twenty yards' distance, without injury to the gallant fellows. It will also, we hope, be remembered that our relation of this incident—clearly showing the advantages of holding on instead of jumping off—was rewarded with a hat, or rather "The Hat." That precious and somewhat remarkable specimen of the wool manufacture of South Carolina is not now in our possession—still is the incident as true as at the first moment of its occurrence.

Taking it altogether, there is no doubt that the Fire Department of New York is superior in point of efficiency as well as in the respectability of its members, to that of any other city of the Union, with the exception, perhaps, of New Orleans, where the Fire Department is admirably organized and conducted. It is almost impossible to over-estimate the services or the importance of these men; and we are ready to overlook, or to regard with leniency, such little irregularities as running upon the sidewalk, and making a little extra noise, in view of the vast and unrequited services of the most arduous and hazardous description, which they are constantly called upon to perform. In Summer and Winter, by night and day, whether it is the palace of the aristocrat or the hovel of poverty which is threatened by the most terrific enemy of life and property in cities, the gallant Firemen are ever ready at a moment's warning to rush to the rescue—to peril their lives and expend their apparently inexhaustible strength and energies for the protection of others. In comparison with the hardships and dangers, the toils and sacrifices, voluntarily encountered by the Firemen of New York, in the cause of humanity, the deeds of the proudest of our warlike legions who have lately been led into a sister nation to burn and lay waste its fair dwellings and butcher its helpless citizens, sink into insignificance, or are only remembered to inspire a just disdain.

Slice XIII.—THE NEEDLEWOMEN.

THE public are already in possession of abundance of statistics on the subject of female labor. Our object at present is to review things in the general, for the purpose of giving the reader a comprehensive view of the various classes into which society in the metropolis is divided. It will be sufficient, therefore, for our purposes to present in a few words the average prices paid for various kinds of needlework, at the principal and prosperous establishments.

Common cotton shirts, and flannel under-shirts, six cents each. A good seamstress can run up two of these shirts per day; and even a very swift hand, by working from sunrise to midnight, can make three; being seventy-five cents per week for the common workers, and \$1.12½ for the swiftest, of course allowing nothing for holidays, sickness, accidents, being out of work, &c. &c. Good cotton shirts, with linen bosoms, neatly stitched, are made for twenty-five cents apiece. A good seamstress will make one in a day, thus earning \$1.50 per week, by constant labor. Fine linen shirts with plaited bosoms, which cannot be made by the very best hands short of fifteen to eighteen hours steady work, are paid fifty cents each. An ordinary hand can make a garment of this kind in two days. Trowsers, overalls, drawers, under-shirts, &c. &c., pay a shilling apiece to the seamstress, who can make one and perhaps two a day. Cloth pantaloons, vests, &c., pay eighteen to fifty cents—very seldom the latter price; and a woman makes, on the average, about one a day. Thus, not to prolong these details, it may be stated, in a word, that the seamstress who is fortunate enough to get steady work earns from seventy-five cents to two dollars a week. Besides these, it is necessary to state that the dressmakers, or at any rate the great majority of them, get absolutely nothing for the work. The way it is managed is this: the proprietors of the large dress-making establishments receive a great number of apprentices, who remain six months for nothing, boarding themselves in the mean time, for the privilege of learning the trade. They can already sew swiftly and well, or they are not accepted. To them are given out the dresses, and they are kept constantly at work sewing (not learning any thing new) until the very day before their apprenticeship expires. Then a few hours are spent in giving them some general directions about cutting a dress, and they are discharged—there being no room for *journeywomen on wages* in an establishment where all work is done by *apprentices for nothing*. As fast as their "education" is completed they are replaced by other apprentices. And so it goes on; the dashing proprietress of the establishment growing rich and aristocratic, and the poor girls turning out upon the world to die of starvation and despair, or sell themselves to infamy.

Here then are the facts respecting a large and increasing class of our female population; and a sad enough picture they present. It is this picture which gave rise a few days since to the following eloquent outburst of feeling from a lady of our acquaintance, of whom I was soliciting information: "Is it not the strangest thing that can well be conceived, that Woman, who by the present constitution of society is made politically and socially a slave—who has no voice in the government to which she submits, in making the laws she is forced to obey—who is in short not recognised by any human institution of these days as an independent individual, or as any thing apart from the necessity Man has for using or abusing her—that she is not, like other slaves whose existence is merged in their masters, even secured food, clothing, and shelter for the fleeting 'gleam between two eternities' on which glides by her pale and suffering apparition! The work-woman has indeed no rights of her own. She can be oppressed, cheated, trampled upon, until the joyous life within her becomes a dead and poisonous impulse that drives her through the world eager for the grave, or stings her into desperation and revenge. But how revenge her wrongs? She has no redress, neither in those laws she did not sanction, nor in that public opinion she cannot influence, and which regards her not. Seeing this, her gentle and tender nature at length undergoes a change. Then the feeble becomes the terrible; the weak and suffering Woman is transformed into an avenging demon. And who may wonder at her?"

In this great republican metropolis—this foregone result of the highest and best thing that civilization can do, with all our boasted "free" institutions in full bloom and life—there are thirty thousand virtuous women who have to live, die, and be buried on what they can earn with their hands. In the ranks of this class of our population, we find Woman in almost every aspect of misery, ever struggling, and faint with the burden of life. Wives and daughters of broken-down merchants and speculating politicians form a large item in this catalogue. Reduced from affluence to poverty and keen want, they are all unlearned in the great secret of yielding gracefully to the inevitable, and maintain day by day a fierce, unequal, but not doubtful contest with "cruel Fortune," until they sink beneath temptation or despair—to the brothel or the grave! A majority are borne up by pride alone from beggary, and the few who still calendar them among their acquaintances do not suspect to what strait they have been driven, until the crisis arrives and is over.

Next come the widows of tradesmen and mechanics, the wives and daughters of those who cannot get employment, and the wives of sick and intemperate husbands, and the children of invalid or drunken parents. Here are to be found some of the most patient and long-suffering, starving, toiling, heart-broken, yet courageous women that ever glorified their Creator. Here, in miserable open garrets, utterly deprived of human hope and sympathy, and often languid and faint from the mere want of food, these creatures show what angels women are. Sometimes—oh! too often—the selfishness of pain and suffering, or the brutal appetite of hunger and intemperance, makes the sick father or the drunken mother command the pale and tender daughter to go out into the streets, and sell herself for gold! Must it not be a life resembling hell itself that begets such crimes as this? And how dare we wonder and shrug our shoulders with a pious sneer at those among these unfortunates who do not resist?

Then, too, from out their workshop windows, through the chinks and crannies of their miserable lodgings, our poor workers see how gayly the busy and seeming-joyous world goes on—how every one appears to have hope in his eye and elasticity in his step. Nor can they fail to mark among the passing throng many women not more beautiful than themselves—whom perhaps they have well known as fellow-workers—who go flaunting idly along in gay and costly robes, receiving the stealthy smiles and admiration of the lords of creation, who follow skulking after till they turn down some dark corner, and with the outlay of a smile and a seductive word secure their victim. They want for nothing—they live in luxury—their white hands look fair and delicate from want of employment—their eyes seem to sparkle with health, and their forms are rounded and elastic with generous fare and absence of toil. Is it surprising that our poor workers, looking out from their rags and squalid poverty and starvation upon all this, should forget (what perhaps they have never been informed of) the horror, the agony, the despair, the disease, the madness, which are the inevitable future of the courtesan? and that too many of them should, alas! desire to be like her?

But we are trenching upon somewhat broader ground than we had intended to occupy in these unpretending sketches, and find ourselves in contact with that great and terrible question, the Causes of Prostitution—a question which none has yet had the courage to answer. Our object is simply to present a correct view of a large and unfortunate class of females, surrounded with all the trials and temptations which beset them—leaving the reader to draw his own conclusions. Having done this, with what little power of pen-limning we possess, we will take advantage of the occasion to solemnly warn young women in the country against indulging for an instant the fatal desire of coming to the City to seek their fortunes by labor. If they could, as we have done, attend day after day the bar of the Police Court, or read the secret docket of the innumerable cases of heart-brokenness, desolation, and crime that there appear, or hear from their own lips the history of the wretched creatures who people the innumerable dens of infamy that abound in the metropolis, they would learn this one frightful truth,—that more than half the prostitutes and female criminals in the city came here from the country to earn a living in some honest way, and to gratify an innocent longing for a little female finery, and a passion to "see the world." The sad story is ever, ever the same: first destitution, then absolute want and hunger, then turned out of doors, houseless and homeless, or offered the dreadful alternative of prostitution. Young Woman!—if you are indeed a real Woman, and no innate demon assuming angelic form of purity the better to carry on hell's work on earth—mark well our warning! Stay calmly where you are, beneath your own pure skies, and amid the virtuous freshness of your home, no matter how humble it may be. Work, spin, dig, till the soil—do *any thing* virtuous that will earn you bread, and mere bread is not so *very* difficult to get in the country! But as you value your moral purity, and the welfare of your immortal soul, come not into the city, to lose yourself in the boiling, seething caldron of licentiousness that rages forever here. If you have an intellect too active to be satisfied with the dull routine of a country life, read and improve your mind by study, and mature your heart by contemplation. If you have aspirations for the beautiful, surround yourself with flowers, and teach birds and gentle creatures to be your playmates and companions; endear yourself to all the little children in the neighborhood: conceive the grand and noble ambition, the only one worthy of Woman's soul, of rendering yourself necessary to your fellow-creatures, within the natural reach of your sphere, and of adding something to the beauty of this beautiful earth, of which God has made you the brightest and most precious blessing. Thus may you, poor and humble though you be, fill your life with a gentle joy that shall bring health and happiness to cheek and eyes, and surround your innocent pillow with celestial dreams.

Slice XIV.—THE PRESS.

Hon. H. Greeley.

Having made our will and got our life insured for a sum sufficient to keep our wife and family in comfortable circumstances after our departure, we are determined to have a dash at the Press. Right or wrong, young or old, handsome or ugly, they shall all traverse the field of our pen-and-ink daguerreotype—*videlicit*, foolscap. But soft—here comes the magnificent nose of our friend Major Noah round the corner. Doubtless his jolly face will shortly follow; and when it, and the burly, Santa Claus-like body which it crowns, shall have presented themselves to full view, you will see selfish good-nature and jolly indifference personified. The Major never was younger than at present—although his reputation was. In the good *old* sleepy days when he acquired a comfortable fame by his *brusque* sallies in the *New York Inquirer* and his neat twinklings in the *Evening Star*, journalism in America was not the absorbing, remorseless, clamorous thing it has become, and a man's brain spread out on a respectably-sized sheet of paper to dry, received somewhat more of respect than a green hide sunning in the Swamp. Then expresses were unheard of, and telegraphs were uncrystallized from the lightning's blue and fiery film—then a happy thought or a happy face were things cherished and recognised by a sedate and unhurried world. But now all this is changed. The little peaceful brook, along whose murmuring banks our friend Noah used to go idling—now stealing a shining pebble and now plucking a pretty wild-flower—has become a roaring and raging river; while the bewildered Major, leaping from knoll to knoll, as the waters encompassed him, has barely escaped with life, and sits out of sight upon a woody bank, hopelessly waiting for the rude stream to run by, that he may resume his old occupations.

Step softly hither and look gingerly through this glass-door—whom do you see? A small, exquisitely built man, with a head swelling out at the temples like an oriental dome—a glorious place to dream in—and an eye restless with the flashing and untameable light of genius, yet apparently subdued to temperate beaming by the sheer power of an overmastering will. That is William Cullen Bryant—the best lyric poet of his land and age; the superior of Cowper in grace and fervor; of Thomson in naturalness and simplicity; of Wordsworth in music and dignity. Yet, with the guerdon of an immortality bright as the stars, within the sweep of his pen-arm, he sits there at one corner of a deal table literally heaped into a mountain of newspapers, uncut books, unread communications, and all the accumulated rubbish of an Editor's table, writing no Hymn to the North Star, but an appeal to Northern voters; no Thanatopsis, but a political thumper for the *Evening Post.* Awake, man, awake! The Philistines are upon thee! Let us see once more the flash of thy pen, and hear the musical thunders which follow!—While there are good ten score who can beat thee all to pieces at political lying, if thou wilt but assume thine own immortal lyre, the world shall be mute to listen.

Let us climb these dark and tortuous stairs—almost as twisted as the course of the journal below—and look in upon this surly, respectable-looking old gentleman figuring up election returns at a table furnished with a case of little drawers, each labelled with the name of a State. In these drawers, neatly scissored, lie the political statistics of each State for many years back. Whatever may be thought of the intertwistifications of the editorial department of the *Journal of Commerce,* Mr. HALLOCK's figures are almost as accurate and reliable as Mr. GREELEY's.

In yonder elegant mansion, where Beauty and Wit and Fashion have made their home, sits in his elegant study the surviving spirit of Lang & Turner's *Gazette*—who, wisely perceiving that it was ebb-tide with the fortunes of the *Gazette,* and that the respectable old craft would inevitably be left high and dry, while all the world went out to sea, had the courage to leap back at once into his old profession, in which he has become the pioneer to what he considers vast and momentous discoveries. The representative of an old and exploded phase of Journalism, has now become the active and enthusiastic exponent of Young Physic. Few remember, when they meet his benevolent face, that he was once nothing but an Editor; and we hope to be pardoned for thus recalling himself to his remembrance.

Another up-stairs journey—having found our way down to the level of Wall-street—will conduct us to the "Editors' Room" of the *Courier & Enquirer.* One Colonel is of course out of town, another—a bland, benevolent-looking gentleman of the old school—is seated on one side of a long, dingy table, hammering out a Money Article. Opposite sits a frail, pale, student-like man, boring into the organ of Causality with the forefinger of his left hand, and scratching away fearfully at a political leader, which is to abolish at a blow Mr. Van Buren, *The Tribune* and Free Soil, and send General Taylor into the White House by Telegraph. A noticeable young man is this—who by the power of a bitter, unrelenting, unrelaxing industry, has made himself, against nature and his own inclination, a Politician and a Journalist in the space of time usually occupied by young men in getting ready to learn.

But we must leave daguerreotyping to another day, and say something in the general about a most interesting and ill-understood class of the community—the regular journeymen Daily Journalists. In any other city of the United States the newspapers are pretty much all alike—apparently run in the same mould, printed on the same paper, with the same type, and having a sort of homogeneous physiognomy, which betrays their origin the instant they are pealed. In New York, however, the Press has as many idiosyncrasies as journals, and each sheet possesses an individual and well-defined existence, scarcely resembling, in its general features, any of its neighbors. One of the most striking peculiarities of the New York journalist is, that he is able to appreciate and assimilate himself with these peculiarities, and to write in turn for all the papers without once forgetting himself or compromising the character of the columns to which he happens to be contributing. Talk of the power of abstraction and individualization in Shakspeare—what is it, compared with the same power as manifested by the accomplished New York journalist? It was comparatively easy to put appropriate words into the mouths of Miranda, and Prospero, and Hamlet, and Cleopatra; but suppose your Shakspeare had been called upon to hammer out a leader for the *Courier & Enquirer* on Monday; condense an almanac for the *Journal of Commerce* on Tuesday; revolutionize Cuba for the *Sun* on Wednesday; prove in the *True Sun* of Thursday that Martin Van Buren was no Democrat; conduct the country through a "tremendous crisis" in the *Herald* on Friday, and correct *all* the blunders of the *Express* for *The Tribune* on Saturday—to say nothing of spinning out half a dozen yards of gutta percha for the *Evening Post*, making hourly observations on the state of the mercury for the *Commercial*, and treating the subscribers of the *Evening Mirror* to mock turtle with their muffins—what think you the world would have ever heard of the Bard of Avon? And yet there are at least half a hundred journalists "attached to the press" of New York, any one of whom could do all this, besides finding time, at odd spells, to contribute a couple of columns to the *Sunday Dash*, write a love-story for the *Sky-blue Magazine*, carry on a daily correspondence with two or three papers at the South or West, and get up a prize tragedy or a satiric poem, according to the state of the market. Indeed the amount and variety of intellectual and physical labor performed by a thorough-bred New York journalist is unparalleled and incredible.

If we attempted to classify the journalists, we should simply divide them as they do almonds and Baptists at the South, into hard-shelled and soft-shelled. The former know how to make the most of their position: the latter allow their good-nature too often to run away with their interest as well as their judgment—and might as well have no pockets.

As a general thing, the habits of the Journalist are very *regular*—he being regularly employed till two o'clock in the morning, and rising at ten the next day to breakfast on hard eggs and cold biscuit. As to "domestic felicity," "keeping wholesome hours," and all that sort of thing, he has read of them, to be sure; but so he has of the diamond valley in Sinbad—and that's all he ever knows about them. His wife and children get perhaps a glimpse of him, for the first time in the week, on Saturday morning—provided the foreign steamer doesn't (which it generally *does*) happen to arrive on that day. His brain, from the effects of constant pumping and squeezing, is very much in the condition of a well-sucked orange; through which dribbles an ocean of the highly-concentrated essence of old-newspaper, in "one weak, washy, everlasting flood." Law, cookery, political and moral ethics, engineering, war, watermelons, tremendous squashes and farmers' clubs, daguerreotypes, washing-machines—are all legitimate subjects of his pen; and some of the finest things he does are upon the incalculable advantages of the baby-jumper and the danger of a national debt. Physic, architecture, music and millinery, are also topics upon which he is completely at home; and as to reviewing books, clairvoyance is no touch to him.

If a new notability from Europe arrives in the City he had better, as soon as possible, put himself on good terms with the hard-shelled journalists. For, talk as we will of the want of influence of the journal and journalists who practise the depleting system upon strangers, yet it is unquestionably true that the slights and sneers, or even the silence, of those papers which are mostly devoted to affairs of theatres, concerts, and public shows of all sorts, are so serious a drawback upon the success of any artist, that we have never known but one (Mr. Macready) to work his way against them. A dishonest journalist is the most active and virulent of mineral poisons, whose venom circulates from the brain (the Press) to the remotest extremities of the social system; and it follows, on strictly homeopathic principles, that nothing but a metallic remedy can prove an efficient antidote. Thus far, we believe, gold has been tried with unwavering success; and contrary to the sister principle established by Hahnemann, that the smaller the dose the more certain the cure, it has been ascertained, in the most marked cases of malignant journalism, the larger the amount of the golden remedy exhibited, the more rapid and satisfactory were the effects. We have known a patient who had reached the last stage of vituperation and actually foamed at the mouth, to be cured by this medicine in a single day.

Your soft-shelled journalist, now, is much more easily managed. A private dinner and plenty of champagne at the Hotel de Paris or at Delmonico's, with a liberal allowance of extra tickets, are generally sufficient; or, if there is a lady in the case, an established footing at the morning levées and the *entrée* of the green-room will generally be quite sufficient. The soft-shelled journalist is of a good heart and is easily delighted. If a performance is not every thing that might be wished, he conveniently remembers that "Art in America is but in its infancy;" and if an unsuccessful engagement has been crowned with a meager farewell benefit, the soft-shelled duly informs the town in the morning that "an audience, although not very numerous, yet unusually fashionable and intelligent, testified their delight," &c. &c.

All this, we are aware, is not entirely creditable to the profession of journalism—nor do we mean to say that there are not exceptions to what we have been portraying. But the general accuracy of our limning, as applied to a majority of the subordinates upon the Daily Press, will be recognised by all who are familiar with the subject. Nor are the journalists themselves so much to blame for this; much of it is owing to a false system—or perhaps is an incurable incident of the profession itself. The writers for the press, as a class, are men of refined tastes, costly ambitions, and high intellectual endowments—they must be so. They are also generally well married, to women of breeding, and partaking largely of the universal female desire *to shine*. Now, what is the scribbler with his expensive appetites and his extravagant family, to do upon his modest salary? True, with economy it would support his family in comfort and respectability. But he is daily obliged to mingle with men of large incomes—politicians, merchants, professionals, and gentlemen—and his position gives him admission to a rank in society far above him in point of money, but probably as much below him in every other respect. If he is shrewd and mercenary, he knows how to sell his influence to the best advantage, and to reap solid benefits from his labors: if merely conscientious and good-natured, he accepts, almost unconsciously, such slight alleviations of the social isolation in which his barren income places him, as tickets to places of public amusement, and now and then a good dinner, can afford.

The truth is, then, that by the system on which the Press is at present conducted, the journalist is hardly treated, considering the character of his labors and the requirements necessary for him to possess. There is no profession in society which demands such peculiar, such diversified, such almost universal natural endowments, and none requiring so much experience and arduous and incessant labor; nor is there any that is, comparatively speaking, so poorly rewarded. This state of things is the consequence of a mutual error between employer and writer. The former, if he could see his own best interests, would not hesitate to remunerate his writers in such a manner as would enable every one employed upon his journal to devote the entire of his time and energies there and nowhere else—to support himself and his family in decency and without embarrassment, and to avoid all the humiliating shifts to which he is now obliged to resort to keep his head above water. An establishment would thus be surrounded with an intellectual cordon that would render it impregnable to the rivalry of new enterprises, and which would impart daily new force and momentum to it, and confer upon it that substantial consistency which most journals in this country so greatly lack. On the other hand, the journalists themselves, by combination and mutual good understanding, might aggrandize their position without doing injustice to employers; might grapple with Fortune by the arms instead of hanging on by the eyelids, and convert their occupation from a precarious struggle for bread into the most noble, the most worthy, and the most useful of the professions. At the same time they should learn to reform many of the bad habits which they have insensibly acquired—to set a proper value upon money—to repress extravagance either in themselves or families—and to avoid, as a pestilence, DEBT, that gulf in which so many high-spirited and intellectual men have lost their footing and floundered and struggled through a disgusting existence.

Slice XV.—THE LITERARY SOÍREES.

HUSH! Open the door softly, after you have smoothed your hair with a pocket-comb which you purchased yesterday at "a cent a pair" of the little girl in Park-row, and adjusted your cravat by the little mirror which Leary has ingeniously inserted in your hat-crown. Step in gingerly and make your respects noiselessly to the smiling hostess, lest you interrupt what is going on in the front parlor, where a dozen distinguished-looking men and twice as many women, whom the veriest greenhorn would at once set down as leaders of the *Bas Bleu*, are gathered in a somewhat picturesque group, listening to a tall, deaconly man who stands between two candles held by a couple of sticks summoned from the recesses of the back-parlor, reading a basketful of gilt-edged notes. It is the Saturday night after the 14th of February, and this is the annual Valentine Party, to which all the male and female authors have contributed for the purpose of saying on paper charming things of each other, and at which, for a few hours, all are gratified with the full meed of that praise which a cold world is so chary of bestowing upon its literary-cobweb spinners. The gentleman to whom has been delegated the task of reading these delicate effusions is a stalwart, middle-aged, puritanical-looking personage, who reads with a clear voice and pure intonation, but with a sort of inflexible solidity, beneath which the filagree verses seem to bend and writhe as if on the point of snapping into annihilation. He has been selected on account of his classical accent and the refreshing distinctness of his articulation. All that is wanting is that the thought-squadrons of Milton, bristling with the chain-armor of genius and inspiration, should be issuing from out the massive portal of his lips, instead of this light holiday procession of dapper fancies, of which he almost seems to be ashamed. This worthy knight of St. Valentine is our friend, the getter-up of innumerable things for the annuals and magazines, and the leading editor of the ——————— the bitterest and most relentless of the extant organs of Conservatism. Mr. ——— is a man of great intellectual strength, but it is muscular rather than nervous, ponderous rather than apprehensive. He looks steadily but in one direction, while the whole world sails by and disappears behind him. He is the oarsman who never sees aught but what he has passed over. The future (we don't mean in another world) is a blank to him. He goes little into society, and spends most of his time at home or at the office, engaged arduously in the duties of his profession. He has betrayed in his writings little of that electric force of genius which beamed from the canvas of his painter-brother Henry —but if he is never great he is always respectable, and never descends to mere puerility.

Stalking about with an immense quarto volume under his arm, (it is an early copy of his forthcoming "Female Poets of America,") is a thin, nervous man, his gray eyes looking shyly about like a girl's, and his mouth twitching every now and then, with the conception of a new biography. He carries his head ponderingly upon his shoulder, as if there were a good deal in it—and so there is; for his room in the University is crammed full of books, and he has managed somehow to absorb the contents of most of them into his own brain. In literary topography he is a peripatetic gazetteer. He knows when every book or other intellectual bantling in America was born, who was its father, (or mother,) how old it was when it died, how many teeth it had, and of what money or other effects it died possessed. He is as familiar with the pedigree of every tyro and blue-stocking, from the Fredoniad down, as a Virginia turfman with that of his stable. His memory is a miscellaneous storehouse of celebrities of whom nobody has ever heard, and of great poetesses who didn't know how to make dumplings. He is the most unselfish of mortals, and has dwelt so much amid the excellences and perfections of others that he scarcely retains cognizance of his own identity. Yet is he, by nature, the equal and the superior of many whom his protection has warmed into vitality. He is a poet of no mean powers, a critic of fine taste and appreciation, although a great deal too good-natured, and a logician of very respectable calibre. Besides these, he is something of an orator and a good deal of a rhetorician; and we have heard of people being profitably exercised under the influence of his "stated preaching."

If his books are neither perfect nor strictly impartial, yet they are incomparably the best of the kind that have been produced; and it is entirely

through them that a host of American writers are known in Europe, who would otherwise have been unheard of. Whatever may be thought of the critical justice of Dr. Griswold, we cannot deny that his labors have been of incalculable benefit to the Literature and Literary Men of his country, and that they form the only accessible or reliable authority respecting a good deal of our national intellectual development.

On the sofa, with his plump, handsome feet piled up on the footstool, and his round face illuminated by a pair of green spectacles, above which rises rather conceitedly and knowingly a capacious brow, buttressed by two very respectable organs of ideality, sits a gentleman listening earnestly to the reading of the Valentines, fearful lest, by some unaccountable mishap, he should have been overlooked. Beside him is a handsome, intellectual-looking young man, evidently of the old aristocratic Knickerbocker blood, who seems to be watching for *the* Valentine quite as intently as his companion. He, however, has no misgiving—he knows it will come—for he wrote it himself, lest his friend should be forgotten. These two personages are in some respects remarkable. Both are men of high intellectual powers—one of them entirely ambitious and ready to dispute his rights on the instant with any rival or pretender; the other as entirely and eminently unselfish—thinking ever only of his friend and how best to promote his interests and advance his fame. They are the Castor and Pollux of literature—the Gemini of the literary Zodiac—the Damon and Pythias of the drama of real life. One of them has produced books which have at least been read, and have furthermore received the compliment of being heartily abused. The other does not write books, but he is a delicate appreciator of the books of others, and for a certain kind of amiable and tender criticism has no rival. Both these men—for they are never apart—form a work in two volumes well worth the studying.

But a polka has struck up in the next room, and we will take a look at the dancers. Here is a sunny-faced, smiling gentleman, who don't look as if the Ink-Fiend had ever heard of him, standing up with a demure lady who has evidently spilled the inkstand over her dress and then had it dyed, so that it should be all one color. The gentleman cannot stand still, but capers and prances about with an exuberance of animal spirits like a racer before the drum beats. At length the time comes; and, shaking his head like a Newfoundland dog about to leap into the water, away he plunges, carrying his partner with him into the dismaying depths of the dance and fairly trampling time out of the music and kicking it into eternity—while his merry and infectious laugh lights up the room with mirth. By-and-by, when the dance is over, he will take you into the wine-room, and tell you confidentially a side-shaking anecdote, which will make its appearance in the "Gossip" of next month's *Knickerbocker.* A joyous, happy spirit is he; and, bating a little unnatural bitterness towards Puffer Hopkins, one of the best-natured, best-hearted, and capitalest fellows in existence. We do not dare to mention his name, for fear of offending his modesty; but if anybody should ask you what kind of a man is Lewis Gaylord Clark, you may show him this paragraph for your answer, and you'll not be far out of the way.

The ladies are scattered all about as thick as stars; yet we do not know how to approach them. There is the stately Mrs. Seba Smith, bending aristocratically over the centre-table, and talking in a bright, cold, steady stream, like an antique fountain by moonlight; and yonder, nestled under a light shawl of heraldic devices, like a bird escaped from its cage, and already longing to get back again, is the spiritual and dainty FANNY OSGOOD, clapping her hands and crowing like a baby. Next her sits, as quiet as a pet lamb, the sedate and handsome Mrs. ———, her tender blue eyes humid with the light of some brilliant fancy she has just been caging. If she were not in Rome, you might see on the opposite side of the table, Miss FULLER, her large gray eyes lamping inspiration, and her thin quivering lip prophesying like a Pythoness. Yonder by the fireplace sits the dark-eyed and poetic-faced GRACE GREENWOOD, talking earnestly, and casting bright glances of lambent defiance around her, as if she loved yet contemned everybody. Behind her, in a low armchair, which sways gently to a half-murmured tune, sits the heart and soul of tenderness and poetry, in the plump and temporal person of LYDIA MARIA CHILD. She never leaves her own retreat; and sings ever loudest and sweetest from her nest. It is strange that we should have encountered her here amid this gay parade of beauty and distinction. Though well deserving place anywhere, by virtue of the depth and purity of her genius, her fervid and o'ermastering worship of the Beautiful, and the sincerity and classic simplicity of her soul, yet she all too seldom strays from home, and seems even now to be uneasy and restless, as if she fancied the room about to compress and flatten everybody in it—and she detests flat people.

Among such a party as this it may well be imagined that conversation flows and sparkles incessantly, and that eleven o'clock (the hour for breaking up) comes unbidden, unexpected, and unwelcome, and without any one having noticed the absence of those stores of eatables and drinkables with which some parties attempt to enliven or beguile their immitigable dulness. Our company drops off one by one, without formal leave-takings, and without creating the slightest confusion. Notwithstanding that all these people spend their lives in endeavoring to attract the attention of the public, yet there is not one of them who wouldn't shrink in dismay from the idea of creating a sensation in a drawing-room. Between the confidence of the author and the self-possessed assurance of the man or woman of fashion, there is a space which is seldom passed over; and it is true as a general thing, that artists and authors are in private life distinguished for nothing but a quiet and reserved demeanor.

These weekly literary *reunions*, of which during the Winter season there are three or four every week among the different literary coteries, are a peculiarity of New York society, which has not been imitated elsewhere to any considerable extent—simply because the materials are wanting. New York, as the grand intellectual focus of the country, is the point at which concentrate the wandering rays of genius from all quarters; and our fashionable *salons* will soon outvie even those of Paris and London in the number and quantity of the choice spirits who congregate within them. It is this which adds the final embellishment and imparts the crowning charm to New York society—which sets a seal of unapproachable value, and confers indescribable force upon New York public opinion, before whose dicta the mind and intellect of the whole country unconsciously bow. It is true, that a certain bitterness and exclusiveness of sectarianism prevail in some other cities, whose inhabitants seem to think it an imperative duty to decry New York. But they deceive themselves as to the facts. Their jealousy and ill-will are not returned by New York. She can afford to appreciate and admire every thing and everybody of eminence or excellence; and the absorbing process by which a new man or a new beauty instantly becomes merged, like a drop of new rain in the river-wave, is entirely unconscious to herself, and arises solely from her own inherent elements of power and greatness. In Civilization every powerful nation must have one intellectual centre, as every individual must have a brain, whose motions and conceptions govern the entire system. In the United States, New York is that centre and that brain.

Slice XVI.—THE OMNIBUSES.

Lounging at our ease in spacious carriages, and reclining on luxurious velvet cushions, we are whirled at will up and down the length and breadth of the City—now dashing through Broadway, half dislocating our necks in trying to get a sight of the gaudy panorama of the "two-shilling side," or endeavoring to get a peep through the interlacing tree-tops at the City Hall clock. Anon we go rattling up Chatham-street and the Bowery, at a killing pace,—especially if there be any small children or "slow" pedestrians in the way—or undulate away through East Broadway into the quieter and cleanlier realms of drab and sober propriety—or jumping into a Kipp & Brown, win our way by gentle "stages" to Greenwich and Abingdon-Place—and all this for absolutely six and a quarter cents a ride. No coach-house, no horses and coachmen to provide for—no waiting for your carriage to come to the door—no bills for feed and fodder—many-caped surtouts with bright buttons,—and all the perplexing *et ceteras,* by means of which unfortunate rich people are compelled to buy their locomotion. It is true, that in the enjoyment of our beautiful Carriage for the Million, we are sometimes, especially in a sudden shower, or just after the locking-up of Wall-street, apt to be somewhat inconveniently crowded; and no regular omnibus-rider is without his established list of complaints against whatever line he happens to be patronising. The Knickerbocker creeps, the Empire races, the Waverley always takes in a regiment of children, the Twenty-third-street stops at every corner. And so the Grumbler—who will always grumble, let what will come of it, and who would grumble if he were going to be hanged—still is not thwarted of his grumbling by the considerate omnibus.

But how few of us, who save annually so many hundred furlongs of weary walking, and so many pounds of costly sole-leather, by the omnibus, ever pause to think of what a blessing we are enjoying, or to ask ourselves the unanswerable question, How should we get along without them? It is true that the now-and-then intermission of a route, for a few days, by reason of fire or other calamity, sets the town to thinking, and we have immediate ways and means set afoot in all feasible modes, to assist in re-establishing the missing utility. Cheerfully we pay a shilling a ride, for a whole day, and never once prolong our walk for the purpose of evading the extra sixpence, when we know that the fund is to go to the benefit of the burnt-out omnibus concern. Our young gentlemen who live on "the western side of the City," purchase theatre-tickets at five dollars apiece to rebuild the Chelsea stages, and thus preserve their patent-leathers. Then it is that we learn to look upon omnibuses in their true light, of a beneficent institution

in the profits and advantages of which the public have infinitely the better of the proprietor. Then it is that ladies who live "a good piece up-town," and whose husbands have not yet discovered a gold-mine, become sensible of the inestimable advantage of this cushioned economy in transmitting them, unrumpled and unsoiled with travel, to the heart of heartless Broadway, to butterfly it of sunny afternoons. Then, too, weary bankers and jaded speculators have leisure, as they jostle home to a cold dinner, and disconsolately read in the *Evening Tribune* that Fancies have fallen, when they should, according to the leader of the *Courier and Enquirer,* have gone up, to reflect upon the reason they have for being thankful that the Knickerbocker line is still "going up—right up"—and that they are not compelled to walk the shine from their boots, and the last ray of endurance from their hearts, ere they can ring at their own door-bells.

Would you like to know something of the Statistics of Omnibuses? You shall be gratified. We have here in New York three hundred and fifty of these locomotive conveniences, coming into the City from every avenue, and all concentrating in the funnel-spout of Broadway below the

Park. You pick your teeth on the Astor House steps, and see, on an average, fifteen omnibuses pass each way, every minute, and for the greater part of the day, all full. Each stage makes ten trips a day, and takes in an average of twenty passengers, up and down. Here are 70,000 sixpences, or four thousand three hundred and seventy-five dollars per day, paid for omnibus riding in the City of New York—amounting to over a million and a quarter per annum. How these sixpences count up when added together by thousands!

There is plenty of philosophy in omnibus-riding, if you have but the wit to find it out. The omnibus is an excellent school for studying human nature, besides being (in the present state of Broadway) an almost sovereign remedy for the dyspepsia. Each division of the day has its distinctive class of omnibus-riders. In the early morning, before the slumbering dust has found its wings, and while the fresh sunlight streams in rosy coolness over the many-dreaming city, the omnibus is chiefly occupied by junior clerks with big iron keys in their hands, or laborers with tin kettles between their feet, on their way to their down-town avocations. All is perfect equality in the early omnibus. The clerk of Jones, Smith, Brown & Co. is not a whit bigger man than the prosperous house-builder in his straw hat and lime-colored *blouse.* Each pulls the strap and pays his sixpence with the same air of absolute independence and equality. The distinction between *ouvrier* and *bourgeois,* if it exist at all, does not reach the sunrise omnibus. If there be an aristocrat about the establishment it is unquestionably the driver.

Later in the morning creep out, one by one, the sleek and rotund burghers of Above Bleecker, who stand imposingly half-way down their palace-steps, and wave their hand with ludicrously majestic motion as the inevitable vehicle heaves in sight. Their linen, how white! the polish on their boots, how unimpeachable! the cheap nod and economic smile with which they statelily greet each other, as rivals meet upon the yielding sofa, and state the fact that it is a fine morning—how indescribably descriptive of the race of whom they are but isolated types! And then when they pull up at Pine or Cedar or Wall-street, they never condescend to even *look* "season" at the driver, but swing open the door as if it were the entrance to their own magnificent dining-room, and descend cautiously picking their way to the sidewalk, with a dainty, three per cent. a month dignity, quite awful to behold.

After these—and not long after them, either—come the fluttering morning robes and thick green veils of Gotham's fair wives and daughters, on their various errands—all muffled inscrutably from sight, and as careful of being seen as the inmates of the harem. It would be so vulgar to be caught in Broadway in the morning! The strap is delicately pressed by the smallest hand in the world, in a ravishing brown thread glove, that clings in pure love to the exquisite proportions it does not conceal; and they disappear upon their various errands—one to visit her milliner or dressmaker, to see every thing in train for the coming party; another to the dentist, to work concealment of the ravages of time and hard tooth-brushes, those moths of woman's smilingness; some to seek slippers, some bouquets, some to cheapen calicoes, and some to buy.

But midday is here; and with it comes the poor man's dinner hour,—and, weary with work, right glad is he to rest and ride half an hour for a hard-earned but blithely-spent sixpence. And now the tide of travel, which since morning has been ebbing strongly towards the sea, begins to set landward. Soon the brokers and merchants, those who have not dined at Brown's, begin their homeward journey, and are followed by a gradually increasing crowd of all occupations, until at sundown it becomes a throng, and you cannot procure a seat—not even a standing-place on the steps—anywhere above the Bowling Green——Fountain, we had almost said—for love nor money.

After this grand supper-time rush, comes a calm, when the foot-passenger almost begins to flatter himself that he is to escape utter deafness; and we next see our friends the omnibus-drivers, with their huge machines drawn up in extempore barricades across the street at the doors of the theatres and concerts, patiently waiting, on the stage without, the movements of the stage within, smoking their cigars and each other in boisterous good-nature, and cracking their jokes and whiplashes with the same unceasing perseverance. Thus they linger far into the night, and at length straggle along up Broadway, one by one, keeping a keen look-out for stragglers on foot, on either side of the way, and making the midnight ring at every corner with their "Broadway—right up!" and the sharp crackle of the whip.

Slice XVII.—THE EATING-HOUSES.

"Beefsteakandtatersvegetábesnumbertwenty—In*jin*hardandsparrowgrassnumbérsixteen!" "Waiter! Waiter! WA-Y-TER!" "Comingsir"—while the rascal's *going* as fast as he can! "*Is* that beef killed for my porter-house steák I ordered last week?" "Readynminitsir, comingsir, dreklysir—twonsixpence, biledamand cabbage shillin, ricepudn sixpnce, eighteenpence—at the barf you please—lobstaucensammingnumberfour—yes sir!" Imagine a continuous stream of such sounds as these, about the size of the Croton river, flowing through the banks of clattering plates and clashing knives and forks, perfumed with the steam from a mammoth kitchen, roasting, boiling, baking, frying, beneath the floor—crowds of animals with a pair of jaws apiece, wagging in emulation of the one wielded with such terrific effect by SAMSON—and the thermometer which has become ashamed of itself and hides away behind a mountain of hats in the corner, melting up *by degrees* to boiling heat—and you will have some notion of a New York eating-house. We once undertook to count these establishments in the lower part of the City, but got surfeited on the smell of fried grease before we got half through the first street, and were obliged to go home in a cab. We believe, however, that there can't be less than a hundred of them within half a mile of the Exchange. They are too important a "slice" of New York to be overlooked, and strangers who stop curiosity-hunting after they have climbed the big clock-case at the head of Wall-street, haven't seen half the sights.

A New York eating-house at high tide is a scene which would well repay the labors of an antiquarian or a panoramist, if its spirit and details could be but half preserved. Every thing is done differently in New York from anywhere else—but in eating the difference is more striking than in any other branch of human economy. A thorough-bred diner-down-town will look at a bill of fare, order his dinner, bolt it and himself, and be engaged in putting off a lot of goods upon a greenhorn, while you are getting your napkin fixed over your nankeens (we think the cotton article preferable) and deciding whether you will take ox-tail or mock-turtle. A regular down-towner surveys the kitchen with his nose as he comes up-stairs—selects his dish by intuition, and swallows it by steam and the electro-galvanic battery. As to digesting it, that is none of his business. He has paid all liabilities to his stomach, and that is all he knows or cares about the matter. The stomach must manage its own affairs—he is not in that "line."

Not less than thirty thousand persons engaged in mercantile or financial affairs, dine at eating-houses every day. The work commences punctually at twelve; and from that hour until three or four the havoc is immense and incessant. Taylor at Buena Vista was nothing to it. They sweep every thing—not a fragment is left. The fare is generally bad enough—not nearly equal to that which the cook at the Home above Bleecker saves for the beggars, (generally her own thirteen cousins, "just come over.") It is really wonderful how men of refined tastes and pampered habits, who at home are as fastidious as luxury and a delicate appetite can make them, find it in their hearts—or stomachs either—to gorge such disgusting masses of stringy meat and tepid vegetables, and to go about their business again under the fond delusion that they have dined. But "custom," they say, does wonders; and it seems that the fear of losing it makes our merchant-princes willing to put up with and put down warm swill in lieu of soup, perspiring joints for delicate *entrées*, and corn meal and molasses instead of *meringues à la crême à la rose.*

There are three distinct classes of eating-houses, and each has its model or type. Linnæus would probably classify them as Sweenyorum, Browniverous, and Delmonican. The Sweenyorum is but an extension downward of the Browniverous, which we have already described. The chief difference to be noted between the two is, that while at Brown's the waiters *actually do* pass by you within hail now and then, at Sweeney's no such phenomenon ever by any possibility occurs. The room is laid out like the floor of a church, with tables and benches for four, in place of pews. Along the aisles (of Greece, if you judge by the smell) are ranged at "stated" intervals, the attentive waiters, who receive the dishes, small plate sixpnce, large plate shillin, as they are cut off by the man at the helm, and distribute them on either side, with surprising dexterity and precision. Sometimes a nice bit of rosegoose, tender, may be seen flying down the aisle, without its original wings, followed closely in playful sport by a small plate bilebeef, vegetables, until both arrive at their destination; when goose leaps lightly in front of a poet of the Sunday press, who ordered it probably through a commendable preference for a brother of the quill; while the fat and lazy beef dumps itself down with perfect resignation before the "monstrous jaws" of one of the b'hoys, who has just come from a fire in 49th-street, and is hungry, *some!*

At Brown's we get a bill of fare, with the "extras" all honestly marked off and priced at the margin. But at Sweeney's we save our sixpence and dispense with superfluities. The bill of fare is delivered by a man at the door, regularly engaged for that purpose, and is as follows:

Biledlamancapersors.
Rosebeefrosegoorosemuttonantaters—
Biledamancabbage, vegetables—
Walkinsirtakaseatsir.

This is certainly clear and distinct as General Taylor's political opinions, and does away with a great deal of lying in print, to which bills of fare as well as newspapers are too much addicted. The Sweeney, or sixpenny cut, is frequented by a more diversified set of customers than either of the others. It is not impossible to see, here, Professor Bush dining cheek-by-jowl with a hod-man off duty, nor to find a blackleg from Park-row seated opposite the police-officer whose manifest destiny it will be one of these days to take him to quod—unless he should happen to have money enough about him to pay for being let go. The editor, the author, the young lawyer, the publisher, the ice-cream man round the corner, the poor physician on his way to patients who don't pay, the young student of divinity learning humility at six shillings a week; the journeyman printer on a batter, and afraid to go home to his wife before he gets sober; in short, all classes who go to make up the great middle stripe of population, concentrate and commingle at Sweeney's. Yet all these varied elements never effervesce into any thing in the slightest degree resembling a disturbance; for eating is a serious business—especially when you have but sixpence and no idea whether the next one has been coined.

It is true that Sweeney's "is emphatically a sixpenny eating-house"—but you must take care what you are about, or you may as well have dined at the Astor.—Unless you know how it is done, you will be nicely done yourself. If you indulge in a second piece of bread, a pickle, a bit of cheese, &c., &c., your bill will be summed up to you something after this fashion:—"Clamsoup sixpnce, rosebeef large, shilln, roastchikn eighteen, extra bread three, butter sixpnce, pickle sixpnce, pudn sixpnce, cheese three, claret (logwood and water alumized) two shilln—seven shilln." If you wish to dine cheaply, be contented with a cheap dinner. Call simply for a small plate of roast beef mixed, (this means mashed turnips and potatoes in equal quantities.) After you have eaten this frugal dish,—and it is as much as any one really *needs* for dinner,—you may send for "bread, hard," drink a tumbler of cool Croton, pay one shilling for the whole, and go about your business like a refreshed and sensible man.

There is still another class of eating-houses, which deserve honorable mention—the cake and coffee shops, of which "Butter-cake Dick's" is a favorable sample.—The chief merit of these establishments is that they are kept open all night, and that hungry Editors or belated idlers can get a plate of biscuits with a lump of butter in the belly for three cents, and a cup of coffee for as much more—or he can regale himself on pumpkin pie at four cents the quarter-section, with a cup of Croton, fresh from the hydrant, gratis. The principal supporters of these luxurious establishments, however, are the firemen and the upper circles of the newsboys, who have made a good business during the day, or have succeeded in pummeling some smaller boy and taking his pennies from him. Here, ranged on wooden benches, the butter-cakes and coffee spread ostentatiously before them, and their intelligent faces supported in the crotch of their joined hands, these autocrats of the press, and the b'hoys, discuss the grave questions as to whether Fourteen *was* at the fire in Front-street first, or whether it is all gas. Here also are decided in advance the relative merits and speed of the boats entered for the next regatta, and points of great pith and moment in the science of the Ring are definitively settled. As midnight comes and passes, the firemen, those children of the dark, gather from unimaginable places, and soon a panorama of red shirts and brown faces lines the walls and fills the whole area of the little cellar. They are generally far more moderate than politicians and less noisy than gentlemen. At the first tingle of the fire-bell they leap like crouching greyhounds, and are in an instant darting through the street towards their respective engine-houses—whence they emerge dragging their ponderous machines behind them, ready to work like Titans all night and all day, exposing themselves to every peril of life and limb, and performing incredible feats of daring strength, to save the property of people who know nothing about them, care nothing for them, and perhaps will scarcely take the trouble to thank them.

But of all this by itself. The type of eating-house of which we have not spoken is the expensive and aristocratic *restaurant* of which Delmonico's is the only complete specimen in the United States—and this, we have it on the authority of travelled epicures, is equal in every respect, in its appointments and attendance as well as the quality and execution of its dishes, to any similar establishment in Paris itself. We have not left ourselves room in this number to speak in detail of this famous *restaurant*, nor of its *habitués*. It well deserves, however, a separate notice; and a look through its well-filled yet not crowded saloons, and into its admirable *cuisine* will enable us to pass an hour very profitably—besides obtaining a dinner which, as a work of art, ranks with a picture by Huntingdon, a poem by Willis, or a statue by Powers—a dinner which is not merely a quantity of food deposited in the stomach, but is in every sense and to all the senses a great work of art.

Slice XVIII.—THE EATING-HOUSES. No. 2.

Some persons who eat—and they form a pretty large portion of the community—may have experienced a shudder of horror at the freedom with which we sliced up the Eating-Houses. As if we were not at liberty to make free with an old friend! Why, we have lived, man and boy, something over a quarter of a century at the down-town Eating-Houses—being in the habit of breakfasting at Lovejoy's, dining at Brown's, and taking our tea and biscuit at Sweeney's. But a picture is a picture; and in order to give the reader or spectator a correct idea of the subject under treatment, it is necessary to dash in the light and shade with a free hand. Exact portraiture is as common-place as—as—the National Academy; while an artistic representation relieves the mind of the material lumber which oppresses it, and presents nothing but the abstract picture to the eye. Whether we possess the faculty of painting such a picture or not, does not depend on the Eating-Houses—they are as economical and as indispensable as ever.

And now, since we are at the confessional, we are willing to admit that the Eating-Houses are immensely valuable. New York could no more exist without her Eating-Houses, than you, reader, could get along without your stomach. In the Winter, when the days are as short as pie-crust, and one has scarcely time to get to his counting-house before it is time to shut up, what business could be transacted, if the fifty thousand people who do business down-town were obliged to go home for their dinners? The progress of trade and population has driven the dwelling-houses all so far up-town, that if it were not for the Eating-Houses, one meal a day would be all that a business man would have any right to expect. Now, he carries on till a favorable lull occurs—an eddy in the vast *counter*-current that is bearing him on to fortune—and slipping quietly out to Brown's or the Alderman's, refreshes the inward man, and is back again in ten minutes, ready to serve a customer, or make out a bill. Consider that this is done by at least fifty thousand every day in New York, and you will be able to begin to calculate the immense amount of time saved to the mercantile and business community by the Eating-Houses.

If the Eating-Houses are so useful in Winter, they become absolutely indispensable in Summer. The thrifty merchant or tradesman sends his wife and children to board in some cool and sequestered place in the vicinity of the city, (and surely nothing can compare with the facilities of New York in this respect,) and where he can join them every evening after the business of the day is over. But all through the hot and glaring day, he must be in town working, working, working. What would he do without the Eating-Houses? Why, literally, he must starve! And then, what would become of his wife and children? Horrible thought!

Indeed, upon taking a cool and calm view of the matter, we are inclined to believe that, notwithstanding their steaming-rooms and thin soups, it is to the Eating-Houses that New York is in a great measure indebted for that continuous rush of commercial activity around her great business centres, which so strikingly distinguishes her from all other cities. Her geographical position doubtless contributes also to this; but without the Eating-Houses, situated right in the heart of trade, and providing abundant and wholesome meals at a cost absolutely nothing to a business man, compared with the value of ten minutes' time in the middle of the day, neither the mere geographical position, nor the immense pressure of trade, would produce that inexhaustible glow of excitement, that ceaseless whirl of activity, which keeps the wine of life continually effervescing and sending off sparks and scintillations which imbue the very atmosphere with a vital and intoxicating essence—the pungent perfume of gold.

In such extensive establishments as the New York Eating-Houses, conducted with such incredible celerity, and dining hungry men by the regiment, some "noise and confusion" are absolutely indispensable. Just think of it—two or three thousand people going up and down the same stairs, and dining at the same tables, within three hours! Such a scene cannot be imagined by any but a New Yorker. Nowhere else, either in Europe or America, does any thing like it exist. It is the culmination, the consummation, the concentration of Americanism; with all its activity, perseverance, energy, and practicality in their highest state of development. In this view the Eating-Houses of New York rise to the dignity of a national institution, and are well worth the most observant analysis.

As a mere branch of business, too, the Eating-Houses are far from being unworthy of attention. We could point to more than one splendid fortune, more than one magnificent residence "above Bleecker," graced with the presence of some of the most beautiful and most accomplished of the Upper Ten, which have arisen from the honest earnings of the Eating-House, and whose founder began life as the humble commissary of cakes and coffee to the mercantile and business men of New York. And so habituated have some of these men become to active employment, that their well-loaded counter, surrounded with happy and hungry customers, has become a necessary excitement; so that they may be seen any day from twelve to three o'clock arrayed in spotless white apron, and, knife and fork in hand, serving out roast beef, plum pudding, and lobster salad, seasoned with certain standing jokes, which grow better every year, to their less wealthy and less aristocratic customers—while their wives and daughters, lounging gracefully on velvet ottomans, beneath damask curtains, in the aristocratic palace up-town, gravely discuss the delicate questions whose decision is to give laws to the world of Wealth and Fashion!

This picture, although it presents points for the use of the satirist, is yet a profitable and a pleasurable subject of contemplation—as it shows us that in this country *any* man in *any* honest calling, and possessing tact, industry, and perseverance, can establish himself and family in any social position for which their natural faculties may have endowed them—that beauty, and worth, and genius, no matter what may be the circumstances of their birth, nor how they may be sneered at by supercilious parvenus, cannot be withheld, save by themselves, from assuming that rank and exerting that influence to which they are entitled.

Therefore, if we have indulged in a little innocent fun while depicting some of the more striking scenes and peculiarities of the New York Eating-House, we are the last to deny their usefulness, their absolute necessity, as one of the most important elements in that great and astounding whole, New York As It Is.

—Under the head of Eating-Houses it is also proper to mention the Ice-Cream Saloons of Broadway, and the Confectionery Shops in the Bowery and other portions of the metropolis. The Broadway establishments are generally fitted up in a style of exaggerated finery, which has a grand effect from the street, but is a little too glaring and crushing when you are within. At night, when the gaudy curtains, silver paper, and gilded mirrors are highly illuminated by gas-light, the scene rises almost to splendor itself, or at any rate to that which most people are willing to accept for it, and never know the difference. In the sultry summer evenings, every one of these fashionable Ice-Cream Saloons is crowded with throngs of well-dressed men and women, belonging for the most part to the great middle classes; while the establishments in the Bowery are crammed to the very threshold with the b'hoys and their buxom and rosy sweethearts, their veins leaping with the fire of health and youth, and their round cheeks glowing with happiness.

But in the daytime, save now and then some dainty male creature, who happens to be in love, and thinks it would be sacrilege to eat any thing heartier than ice-cream and lady-cake till the crisis comes off, (being fortunately ignorant that his *bella inamorata* is at that very moment "putting in" a slice of roast beef garnished with string-beans and new potatoes,) the ice-cream saloons are mostly patronised by ladies, who stop on their way from Stewart's to regale themselves with a dish of fragrant souchong and a sandwich, or perhaps the more exquisite but dangerous luxury (so fascinating are dangerous luxuries!) of a sherry-cobbler. Here, too, if appetite prompt, they can be supplied with the finest of oysters, delicately served, or with a broiled chicken-wing, a woodcock *à la toast,* or even the more vulgar and substantial luxury of a porter-house steak.

And so, good-by to the Eating-Houses—till dinner-time.

Slice XIX.—DELMONICO'S.

To dine at Delmonico's, as a correspondent of *The Tribune* once said of travelling in Europe, two things are requisite—money and French. Of the latter a little will answer; but the more you have of the former ingredient the better you are off, as well at Delmonico's as elsewhere.

The lower saloon is appropriated to general and indifferent customers, who come in in a hurry and must return to their business as soon as possible. The great and extensive French and continental importing interest furnishes two or three scores of daily dinners at Delmonico's—men of education and refined tastes, familiar with the world and carrying with them wherever they go an air of quiet and easy deference so characteristic of the thorough-bred gentleman everywhere, and which make you at once feel a higher respect for yourself as well as for everybody else. Besides these, you will frequently meet little knots of travelled American gentlemen, who have unconsciously caught the same tone and spirit. The waiters, too, have been regularly trained to their profession, and, without seeming to observe you, are always at your elbow just at the moment you are beginning to think about wishing for something, and listen to you with a grave attention which assures you that you are to receive exactly what you have ordered, and in the shortest possible time. They seem to come by electric telegraph, at the first motion of your thought.

After you have ordered your dinner, (and we don't suppose you to be such a booby as to require any instructions as to what you will eat,) you have a little leisure to look about and make your observations. There on your right is an elderly Frenchman dining with his son. The father is still splendidly preserved, and his hair, whiskers, and moustache have been so exquisitely dyed that their owner himself begins almost to think that he has been only dreaming of the flight of Time. It is really beautiful to see the perfect deference with which the handsome old gentleman is treated by his boy. Whether it is a something in the dignified affability of the father, or the greater reverence of the son, certain it is that the paternal authority sits

much more gracefully and naturally with foreigners than with us. They are no better, perhaps, but they are more gracious. They have had the good sense to think it worth while to study and teach the philosophy of the Little. On this nine-tenths of social happiness depends. This, most American men, and women too, have yet to learn, or at best but selfishly and partially understand.

At the next table behind these, in an attitude of listless self-complacency, sits a tall, striking-looking man, with ruddy beard and moustache, setting off a voluptuous and decidedly handsome mouth. He has evidently just finished—his breakfast; for there stands the gigantic chocolate-cup, deep enough for him, long as he is, to drown himself in it, and before him lie the delicate remains of the *œufs en miroir* with which he has been trifling. Although still under twenty-five, he is evidently a thorough-bred man of the world—an epicure, an amateur, a dilettante, a gallant, a critic, almost a coxcomb. You would think at first that he had travelled. So he has—but it has only been between book-covers. There are few operas he does not know—from the score; few pictures, statues, or churches he is not familiar with—by description; but he has in reality never been out of New York. He is, prejudice, vanity, obstinacy and all, a remarkable young man, and wields an intellectual battle-axe between his thumb and forefingers that will cleave its way in time through any Front-de-Bœuf castle of stupidity that he may chance to fall in with. That is Richard Grant White, the musical critic of a morning paper.

To the right, yonder, nestled among piles of preserve-jars, scolloped oranges and *meringues à la crême,* are four persons somewhat worthy of notice. The one whose profile is turned to us, he with the massive, Jupitolan head and bushy hair—upon whose sensuous mouth good-nature is broadly contending with scorn of every thing and everybody, and nine times in ten gets the mastery—is Parke Godwin; one of the profoundest, most earnest, yet most consistent and practical of our strong men of progress, whom it has been the good fortune of the present age to produce. He is an Associationist, a Swedenborgian, a Homeopathist, a Hydropathist, a —— we know not what. But he is at the same time a hard and hopeful worker in the circle where he finds himself and with the materials which surround him. When men learn to think for themselves, instead of taking the wind from those human weathercocks perched upon high places, they will discover that here is a man who has gone before them—who has thought more than they ever have thought or can think.

Opposite him, in almost every respect, is a tall, shapely man, daintily dressed, and in a style that lets peep out here and there an all-pervading and inextinguishable love for the beautiful, which even, as in woman, seeks to expend itself upon the dress. The upper part of his face, with the long, clustering, glossy ringlets,

"......brown in the shadow, golden in the sun,"

has something cherubic in its expression—but the eye is small and sensual; and the irrepressible pout of the under-lip, and the white, full-swelling throat, add at once mortality to the composition. He is, as perhaps he himself might not disdain to express it, a sort of human julep, composed of spirits and sugar, with a pungent flavor of the mint, which makes the very air spicy around him. On his upper-lip grows modest and maiden-like a brief moustache, delicately arched into a capital W, and which will doubtless in time fulfil its orthographical destiny in completing the name of its owner—Willis.

At the right-hand of the amber-maker, in whose embalming ointment of sweet words straws are preserved till they become precious as diamonds, behold we indeed a manly and a noble face. Not a tortuous nor crossed line on its whole broad and smiling periphery. Even the tracks left by Time's crows as they go croaking over both poet and fair lady, bower and sanctum, have an air of openness and temerity, as if they said, "We spell 40—have you any objection, sir?" His forehead is lofty and unruffled as the glaciered Alps—eyes mild and blue, with the golden dream of poetry shining through and threatening to rain beautiful conceits—mouth bold, decided, utilitarian, anti-poetical and substantial. He speaks slowly, elegantly, and from the purpose—very much as he writes,—yet always with a visible trace running through the mottled web that will be sure to lead him home at last. Sometimes his soul lights with a chivalric new thought—then indeed the painted and wildly-scattered clouds begin to concentrate—and now, look out for a musical thunder-storm! That is CHARLES FENNO HOFFMAN, the song-writer of America: and if he and WILLIS never did dine together at Delmonico's it is not my fault—they ought to have done so.

The fourth member of this group is only an Editor, and not worth wasting time or foolscap upon. No matter what he writes, it will be forgotten to-morrow; while the "cooks wanted" in the advertising page will be cherished at least a week—by the housekeeper. He, however, like the poor ephemeron, seems to be unconscious of the speedy and daily oblivion to which he is hastening, and laughs as heartily as if he had a month of fame to live—deluded man! The leader upon the Irish question in England, which you have been all day ransacking other people's libraries and your own brains to concoct, will be read to-morrow by six old fogies on their way to Wall-street, just to keep them out of speculating on somebody in the omnibus, and will be spelt out, by way of penance, by your unhappy eldest daughter, so that she may praise it to mamma at dinner, and thus swindle you out of money for a new frock.

The rest of the room is occupied by merchants whose thoughts are upon bank accounts and balances, as they attempt to play patient while their meals are coming. They all belong to the same class, and its type it would be difficult to describe. With the exception of moustaches inconveniently long, which seem to be dragging the soup-spoon for dead bodies, they have no salient nor remarkable features. They dine, pay, go away—bargain, sell—do so again to-morrow—and the next, and the next day, and so on from month to month and year to year—never changing, never growing old—never dislocating their jaws nor jerking their heads across the room while speaking, although it seems inevitable that the next gesticulation must produce those results.

Above-stairs are numerous suites of private apartments, embracing sitting, dining, and retiring-rooms—plainly but sufficiently furnished, and kept constantly busy. Into these rooms, perfumed with the fragrant breath of Burgundy, we have no right to enter. Though should we make use of our clairvoyant faculties, now and then, we might discover and relate scenes that would make the fortune of a reporter. When we grow avaricious of fame or money we may attempt it.

Thus have we made the tour of the New York Eating-Houses, to discover that not one of them is conducted on the true principle. By the application of a proper system of co-operation and distribution of labor and profits, all the advantages of Delmonico's could be easily furnished at the minimum sixpence of the others. This will some day be understood by capitalists as well as consumers; and then it will be accomplished at once—while all the world will wonder why they had not thought of it long ago.

Slice XX.—THE DANDIES.

Since the lamentable failure of the whisker-crop on the *Boulevard des Italiens,* New York is the only City and Broadway the only street in which any thing like a respectable assortment of live Dandies can be found.—As to the bucks of Bond-street and the swells of St. James, we regard them not. Never was that peculiar and exquisite compound of genius and folly, nonsense and intellect, necessary to the creation of a perfect Dandy, found in an English skull. We know what you are going to say about Beau Brummel, and Bulwer, and Ben D'Israeli—but that doesn't shake us a jot. They must be regarded as monstrosities—and besides, D'Israeli, who comes much nearer a Dandy than either of the others, is a Jew. In New York, however, we have an abundance of the true mixture—the French sparkle, the Italian grace, the Spanish impudence, and a pretty considerable tall sprinkling of the true "native American nerve." In short, as Paraguay is said by travellers to be the paradise of monkeys, we regard New York as destined to become the metropolis of Dandies.

The first requisite of character for a Dandy must be an affectation of absolute indifference. Dandies must be exactly the reverse of all the rest of mankind; and as common people see so many beautiful and wonderful and melancholy things as they go through this world that their admiration or their sympathy is constantly in a state of excitement, it of course becomes a necessity of existence with the Dandy that he should admire nothing and sympathize with nothing. To maintain successfully this difficult and tedious *rôle* through life, requires certain powers of mind and attributes of character to be immensely developed; and the mere spoony who (like most mere spoonies) attempts to play the Dandy, is very soon discovered to be only the dunce. A genuine Dandy need not have a heart, but he *must* have brains; he need not be profound, but he must be brilliant; he does not require absolute talent or genius, but he must possess inexhaustible invention and gigantic tact. Indeed, to be a consummate Dandy, it is necessary to have been born for a great man and unfortunately shut up in a bandbox by mistake. Extravagance, gaudiness, or peculiarity in dress are the things which, although they almost certainly bespeak the vulgarian, are least likely to indicate the Dandy. Ostentation and superciliousness to inferiors are equally opposed to the idea of Dandyism—which, however it may annihilate its equals or humiliate its superiors by an intense and cool contempt, is careful to treat its inferiors with deference and respect. Perfect, absolute self-possession, at all times and in all places, is the fundamental element, as it is the crowning glory of Dandyism.

In New York Dandyism is already established, and recognised as a permanent element of society; and we can at once put our finger on several magnificently got-up specimens of the different genera of this interesting species.

Among the most interesting, as being the best known, is the Dandy on Short Allowance. This unfortunate creature has but a single object for which to live—an object which employs all his waking thoughts, and presents itself even in his dreams. This is to conceal, not only his poverty, but every thing that might lead to a suspicion of it. Rich men may be mean, without damage to their credit; but the Dandy on Short Allowance must ever appear liberal, at any sacrifice—unless in the case of servants or tailors, or such rubbish. To these he may be—and in fact it is his duty to be—as stingy as possible. He may face his butcher out of a shilling a day and get up false inventories of his linen for the purpose of cheating his washerwoman; he may black his own boots and dine on a link of Bologna sausage and a cracker; he may resort to any economical shift that suggests

itself in the internal economy of his establishment—but he must be liberal before folks. We know of more than one aristocratic and tonnish family who many a time go supperless to bed and wake up hungry, that the head may keep his riding-horse and sport a sofa at Niblo's; and often and often have we heard the champagne pop at his expense, when the grocer on the corner wouldn't trust him for a pint of vinegar.

Well—if he chooses to make such a sacrifice, who shall condemn him? Who does not also play a part, of some kind—fortunately, both for himself and others, if it be any thing so harmless as the innocent self-delusion of the

Dandy? You, General, with cocksfeather on your empty head, and the brass of your cowardice gilded over with the tinsel of your epaulette! what part play you in this great world-drama, that you should sneer and curl up your ugly moustache at our poor Dandy? Or you, learned and fair sir, with watch in hand and finger on pulse! what know you of the sick man's ailing, or of the real properties of the horrent and nauseous stuff you will presently administer to him with an air of pompous and owl-like wisdom? Should he die within the hour, you will carry to the grave the consciousness that you may have killed him—but the world is none the wiser for that. The part you play is that of the great medicine. Only continue to have plenty of impudence, and they will never discover that you were racing on the Avenue when you were supposed to be at your Lectures, and that you became a capital hand at billiards while you might have wasted your time in studying bones and cartilages in the noisome atmosphere of the Dissecting-Room.

But to return to our Dandies. Next in order to the Dandy on Short Allowance comes the Rich Dandy. The animal is rarer, and consequently the fur is esteemed as much more valuable by those who have the plucking of it. The Rich Dandy is an enormous favorite at eating-houses, club-rooms, and gambling establishments, and it is here that he passes most of his life, with the exception of the brief intervals that he allows himself to be importuned by "cotton" mothers and fascinated by irresistible young ladies. Here, however, his very perplexity saves him. Were there but one, he would be hooked in a fortnight—he is so good-natured. But now, he knows not how to choose, and thus break the hearts of all the rest. So the Rich Dandy lives and dies a bachelor—bequeaths his boots to his valet, his wines and pictures (such as will answer for public inspection) to the auctioneers, and his fortune to the Surrogate.—He never does good to anybody, except to the two dozen score of toadies who eat and drink at his expense, and make merry and free with his money. He lives and dies without an enemy—and without a friend; he is less remembered than his dinners, and is mourned for as the sponge laments the fate of the Croton when the pipe at which it fed is turned off.

The Pinchbeck Dandy is the man you saw yesterday "cavorting" up Broadway, with a cane of the size of Hercules' club, his broad plaid trowsers "sixty inches round the bottom," and spread out over the instep so as nearly to conceal his foot. His appearance is generally what is termed "flashy"—but that doesn't exactly describe it. We should rather characterize it as outre and deliberately ungraceful. It is imitated from the cockney idea of gentility, which is to dress, in some way, markedly unlike everybody else. With a man of genius, this ambition, turned in a higher direction, may create a dandy—with a mediocre man it only leads him to become a fool. To seek for notoriety and distinction in the peculiar cut or color of one's clothes, is reducing the idea of man to its minimum dimensions. King Jocko-Bung of the Cannibal Islands, with fish-bones stuck through his nose and ostrich feathers in his ears, sticks his legs through the sleeves of a scarlet coat and struts about, a perfect specimen of the Pinchbeck Dandy.

A great majority of the Dandies of New York, as well as of every other place, belong to this variety. They are the greatest cowards in existence, notwithstanding appearances to the contrary; and a straight-forward look into their eyes will cow them as instantaneously as it will any other impudent puppy. They generally live a worthless, deformed life, and sink down from a disgraceful youth to a mean manhood and a contemptible old age. Their haunts are the grog-shop, the theatre, the bowling-saloon, and the Third-avenue. They are ambitious of being quoted as authorities as to how many pins Joe Noggins got down with ten balls, and how many points at billiards "Andrew" made without stopping. Whenever they make their appearance at any public place frequented by ladies and gentlemen, it is their delight to keep nervous people on the rack for fear of a row—of which, however, there is not the slightest danger. If they are at a Concert, they consider it a capital joke to wear their hats, and make so much noise, with feet, hands, and tongue, that nobody in their vicinity can hear a note of the music. They mostly go in squads; and one of them by himself is always as still as a mouse. In a word, they only lack courage to be the most disagreeable and dangerous of ruffians; but, as it is, they merely rise to the level of third-rate loaferism. On Sundays they range themselves around the doors of fashionable churches, and stare out of countenance such ladies as may be without protection, or are only accompanied by an old man, from whom our bloods would be able to run away should he attempt to chastise them. At night, too, they prowl about the streets insulting poor seamstresses and milliner-girls on their way home with work. Such infamous acts as these sufficiently stamp their character. They are a pest and a nuisance, whom every decent man should be authorized to kick out of his way whenever he encounters them.

Such is a brief *catalogue raisonnée* of the Dandies of New York—a race of beings which will in good time become extinct, to make room for one of the eighteen supplemental races who, according to Fourier, are to make their appearance from time to time upon the earth, as Man progresses in the accomplishment of his destiny. It won't be very hard to spare them.

Slice XXI.—THE LIQUOR GROCERIES.

Of the innumerable dens of dissipation which our City contains, we believe the Liquor Groceries (by which we mean family groceries where grog is retailed) are the most pernicious, because they afford facilities for drunkenness to thousands of husbands, wives, and children, who otherwise might not be tempted. Situated in the midst of neighborhoods thickly inhabited by poor families, whose members are compelled to resort to them daily for the supply of the table, they afford a tempting lounging-place to the tired laborer as well as the vexed housewife, who spend there in drink and hurtful idleness the hours of rest and domestic intercourse. The little remainder of the weekly earnings left over from the bill for groceries and other necessaries from the store, is quickly absorbed for rum and whiskey, while every week of this indulgence renders its victims less able and less disposed to work. The household and the shop are thus neglected—work disappears, confidence in the man's honesty is destroyed, the dwelling is squalid, the children filthy and naked, and soon the most abject poverty steps in—Pauperism conducts the wretched inmates to the Almshouse, Crime hurries them to the Penitentiary, or Disease bears them to the grave.

After the money is gone, the first thought of the drunken father or mother is to pawn the furniture of the house, and when that disappears, their own and their children's clothes, until every thing possessed by the wretched family is swept away—melted into the whiskey-barrel—and utter deso-

lation and destitution reign where once was smiling and full-fed content. The scenes which take place nightly in these filthy holes are enough to make one despair of human nature. On the one hand, the degradation and abjectness of the poor father and mother reduced by a brutal appetite to beggar themselves and children; and on the other, the cold-blooded mercenary grog-seller, careless of the misery and ruin he inflicts upon a whole family, so that he can add a few shillings to his sordid gains, are spectacles inspiring almost equal pity and disgust. If it is necessary to have, as people at present seem to think, a "family grocery" on every corner, there surely is no need that these establishments should deal in liquors, and peddle out poison at three cents a dose. If the stuffs they sold were the genuine liquors whose names they bear, the case would be bad enough; but they are, almost universally, the most villanous and filthy compounds, often containing active and deadly poison. The brandy sold here is nothing but alcohol, tinctured and flavored with various noxious ingredients to give it color and flavor—the gin is mere ratafia and whiskey—the rum is the fieriest New England, sweetened and corrupted—and, as has been proved by abundant experiments, the beer and other malt liquors are composed of the most deleterious and disgusting substances. Armed with such fatal weapons as these, the Liquor Grocery squats itself like a venomous toad upon the corner of a block of miserable poor-men's dwellings, crowded and overrunning with families, deprived of air and wholesome sunshine, and disseminates its venom on all around. It is no wonder that the neighborhood grows filthier and filthier, and its inhabitants more and more besotted and depraved. One after another the men and women become drunkards, their neglected and abandoned children grow up thieves and prostitutes, and the whole vicinity reeks with crime and every uncleanness. But the proprietor of the Liquor Grocery waxes fat and thrifty. One after another the wretched hovels of his pauper customers are stripped of furniture and beds, and even their inmates of clothes, while all comes to his counter in exchange for rum, and is transmuted into silver and golden profits. By and by he begins to expand his ideas and his operations—adds note-shaving and bill-broking in a small way—perhaps advances thirty per cent. on gold watches handed in by seedy-looking customers, without asking any questions as to how they came by them—and eventually swells out into the capitalist and the financier; makes his appearance one fine day in Wall-street among the speculators in the fancies, while his wife and daughters flare out in a fire-new mansion "Above Bleecker;" take a front sofa at the Opera, and affect to rule the world of fashion and aristocracy. As to his customers—from whose madness he amassed his fortune—they have not fared so well. Some are in the Hospital, some in the Almshouse, and others in the Penitentiary or State Prison—while a few of the more fortunate among them are in their graves.

But we have not yet completed our description of the Liquor Groceries. As soon as the shutters are closed at night upon the scenes we have been depicting, another class of operations commences. The cabman, the private groom, the colored steward, the incipient pickpocket, the b'hoy, drop in, one after another, and soon a little knot is formed round the counter. A pack of greasy cards is produced—the sixpences tinkle—the eyes of the host and banker glisten with the shine of his anticipated gains, a game of sixpenny vignt-et-un or penny poker commences, and every heart is absorbed in the one worst, most fiendish passion of the human soul. Thus, all night long the game is kept up, mollified now and then by a choice swig at the "poney"—(all at the expense of the benevolent landlord!)—unless some member of the party gets unusually boozy, or excited with his losses, and breaks up the concern in a grand row. Then enter the Police Officers—"Walk in, gentlemen, and take a drink!" and the offenders are dragged off to the Tombs, and duly reported against in the morning by the order-loving officers, while the landlord sweeps off the money with a chuckle and a wink—sands his sugar, waters his rum, and moistens his tobacco—and after a short prayer,

"——— wraps the drapery of his couch
About him, and lies down to pleasant dreams!"

The Liquor Grocery would not be complete, in its debasing and demoralizing power, without the presence and assistance of those wretched female outcasts, whose breath is pollution, and whose touch leprosy. Accordingly, as soon as night sets in, the groceries in certain quarters of the City begin to be haunted by these wretched beings, who fortify themselves with alcohol for their nightly occupation. It is difficult to imagine a more heart-chilling spectacle than the interior of one of these dark and dingy establishments with a group of gorgeously-dressed women drinking and blaspheming round the counter. When you remember what an angel of purity and goodness Woman ought to be, and then behold the scene before you, the power of contrast is exhausted—Heaven and Hell are as it were spread out to view.

There are yet other evils connected with these petty groceries which well deserve attention. The articles they sell are for the most part inferior, and often positively unwholesome, and the manner of retailing them out by the three cents' worth makes them cost the consumer two, three, or four times as much as the fair market price, and often a great deal more—to say nothing of what sticks to the measure or the scale, nor of the false weights and measures used in too many of these establishments. The swindle thus practised upon the poor man is enormous and incredible. His earnings, meager as they are, would be more than doubled, in effect, if he could buy his groceries and provisions at fair prices and of good quality, instead of frittering away his money for sixpences' worth of butter, half pints of molasses, and tenpenny slices of ham. The grocery keeper, for instance, buys butter of an inferior quality at twelve and a half or fourteen cents per pound, and retails it at two shillings. For half a pound he generally manages, by an ingenious use of ten and five cent pieces and cents, to get thirteen; for a quarter, seven cents; while he boldly puts on the two-ounce weight (with a hole in the bottom) whenever a bare-legged little girl calls for "four cents worth of butter"—thus making the pound bring him thirty-two cents. He buys a barrel of common New Orleans molasses at twenty-five cents per gallon, and retails it to his customers at sixpence the pint—of which one-sixth sticks to the measure—thus bringing the price to the consumer to half a dollar or seventy-five cents per gallon. In liquors it is the same. Whiskey costs the grocer thirty cents per gallon, and he reduces it ten or fifteen per cent. for the sake of temperance. He then retails it at sixpence per half pint, or a dollar per gallon. His brandy costs him, including the expense of coloring and poisoning, from thirty-five to forty cents per gallon, and he sells it at two dollars; or, in case of a customer who wants something very choice, he draws it from another cask of the same kind, calls it "Real Old Cognac of 1800," and unblushingly receives three dollars and a half per gallon for the villanous stuff! And this system is carried through almost every article in the shop. In one corner is a tub of stale distillery milk, ready to curdle with the loathsome diseases with which every particle is rife, and which is sold at five cents per quart, as "genuine Orange County"—in proof of which a rag hangs out at the door with a clumsily-painted cow done in brickdust. By the use of this poisoned milk alone, thousands of infants and children are sent to premature graves —as any respectable physician of experience will readily inform you. The butter, eggs, lard, salt fish, and meat sold here are also generally stale and rancid, unfit to sustain life, and highly conducive to disease, and constantly keeping the neighborhood predisposed to take the first epidemic that arrives, in its worst and most malignant form. These causes, added to the filthy and unventilated apartments into which our poor population is crowded, abundantly account for the devastating virulence with which the cholera and other epidemics sweep through the ranks of the working classes; and when we add the dreadful consequences of dissipation upon poisoned liquors and beer, the picture of horror is complete.

Thus we see that these Liquor Groceries—of which we have some two thousand in New York*—constitute one of the greatest pests and curses of society. Furnishing as they do the facilities of dissipation to the great body of the poorer classes, they therefore deserve the especial and earnest attention of every true friend of temperance. As one such we urge upon the authorities, with all the force of conscience and duty, to discuss gravely in their councils the question as to the right or propriety of granting license to any family grocery whatever to sell intoxicating liquors—at the same time to bestir themselves in suppressing the innumerable holes where it is sold *without* license. Could they, as we have done, go through these vile haunts, and see their miserable victims drinking away their lives and pawning their children's bed and clothing, they would, we are certain, postpone for a time their fierce debates upon the distribution of the spoils of office, forego all considerations of vote-making and political popularity, and set seriously at work to cleanse the City of these dens of pollution and iniquity. Is it too much to ask of a government which costs as much as ours, that it should do what may be done to suppress and extirpate the thousands of pest-houses which scatter death and destruction in our midst? Of what use are our magnificent systems of public education, our splendid private charitable societies, and even the effective efforts of unostentatious individuals of piety and benevolence, when all their benign influences and endeavors are neutralized by the pestilence of a grogshop seated at every poor man's door? What is the responsibility of that government, which, informed and warned of these things, still suffers the evil to continue and increase from year to year? Will a splendid weekly collection in the Tea-Room—even though the reporters are excluded out of tenderness to the dear people's purse—will an annual cherry-party to Randall's Island—a

* A recent examination of the records at the Mayor's Office shows the following number of licenses to sell liquor granted during the present year:

NUMBER OF LICENSES IN EACH WARD.

Ward	Licenses	Ward	Licenses	Ward	Licenses	Ward	Licenses
I	185	VI	182	XI	228	XVI	251
II	85	VII	228	XII	147	XVII	192
III	221	VIII	224	XIII	123	XVIII	171
IV	356	IX	169	XIV	198	Miscellaneous	229
V	201	X	178	XV	120		
Total number							3,688

Of this number there are perhaps about five or six hundred who take out licenses for regular and respectable hotels, and for excise. These of course do not come within our descriptions of "*Liquor Groceries.*"

Fourth of July jubilation—a grand turn-out and flare-up to the tune of five or six thousand dollars every time Brevet Drum-Major John Smith honors the City with a visit—will all this serve to cover up these momentous moral delinquencies, of which they are doubly guilty, as magistrates and men? and if so, how is it with them as Christians?

Slice XXII.—THE IMMIGRANTS.

THIRTY-TWO thousand seven hundred and odd Immigrants arrived in New York during the month of May. In June thirty-three thousand and forty-seven, and in July, August, and September, the number will probably be increased to forty thousand per month; while during the Winter there will probably not be so many. Taking the whole year together, we may estimate that we shall receive an addition to our population from Emigration alone, of some three hundred thousand souls, at this single port. Of this immense mass of human beings less is known than of any other class of inhabitants—partly from the indifference which all feel about what does not immediately concern themselves, and partly from the difficulty of obtaining reliable information. Until the passage of the recent law respecting the licensing of immigrant runners and agents, there were over seven hundred persons engaged in the business—many if not most of them making large sums of money by deceiving, lying to, and swindling the poor Immigrants, under all sorts of scandalous pretexts. The main business, however, was decoying them into cheap boarding-houses, and then extorting extravagant prices until their money was nearly gone, and finally defrauding them of the remainder by a forged ticket of conveyance through to Buffalo, St. Louis, Chicago, or wherever else they wished to go, and which would only take them up the river as far as Albany, or some intermediate landing—where they would be left utterly penniless and destitute on the shore, without a friend and with no possible means of redress, often being unable even to speak a word of our language. It is horrible to think of the hundreds of innocent and confiding people, willing to work, and who have sought this land of liberty under the impulse of a sentiment of admiration and confidence, which of itself adds nobility to their character, thus plundered and left utterly helpless to starve or beg. No wonder they do not all turn out models of intelligence and patterns of propriety.

The "emigrant boarding-houses" into which these people are inveigled upon their arrival here, are for the most part tolerably fair buildings and decently kept, but many of them are the vilest and most abominable sties ever inhabited by swine. They are generally located in the streets nearest the wharves on either side of the city—built of brick and in the narrowest and most sordid fashion—utterly destitute of wholesome space in rear, dry cellarage, or needful ventilation—cut up into little rooms, or rather stalls, floor above floor, into which whole families are thrust to swelter and corrode and grow abhorrent—overrun from basement to garret with cockroaches, fleas, bedbugs, wharf-rats, and every other sort of vermin indigenous or possible to the climate, and never cleansed from the time they are built until they tumble down.—In the ground story is generally a "family grocery and provision store," supplied with a few maggoty hams and shoulders, half-a-dozen bunches of lard candles melted into one, some strings of dried onions, a barrel of No. 3 mackerel, some pipes and tobacco, and above all two barrels of whiskey—one colored red with oak-juice and sold for "first-rate Cognac brandy," and the other answering with the most limpid assurance to the various demands for gin, Monongahela, or schnapps.—Down cellar there is a cooper's-shop, a "fence," or a coal-yard, and in front you can buy for sixpence stale oysters more than you would eat for an eagle.

For the "apartments" in these delectable dwelling-places various prices are demanded, according to the size of the immigrant's pile, from three dollars down to fifty cents a week—which must be paid, like the subscription to a new paper, "punctually in advance." The great source of profit, however, to the keepers of these establishments is the "store." Here whiskey which costs twenty-five cents a gallon, is dealt out at sixpence the half-pint, (with a thundering big thump in the bottom of the measure, all for the good of the Temperance Cause,) and molasses is dribbled away by the three cents-worth until it costs the consumer a dollar and a half a gallon. In such economical expenditure and such sumptuous temptation, of course the immigrant's money soon finds the level of the money-drawer, in the "grocery," no matter in what story he may lodge.

In one of these wretched abodes we saw a scene, not many days since, which can no more be forgotten than the pain of an insulting blow. In one of the little filthy rooms we have mentioned, up three flights of stairs, were an entire immigrant family—the young, stout-hearted, lithe-limbed husband and father, now bowed to the dust in unutterable wo, as he tried in vain to weep over the body of his wife, who had died an hour or two before with that terrible immigrant-scourge the Ship Fever—while a little child, its large blue eyes yet reflecting the heaven whence it had so lately come, and its white skin as soft and pure, amid all the desolate filth around, as rose-leaves, lay laughing and playing with the stiff and clammy tangles of its dead mother's hair. There was—except the face of this unconscious child—not one feature to relieve the scene of complete, squalid, desolate wretchedness, or to invest it with that decent dignity which alone has claims upon the sympathies of well-bred benevolence: nothing, on either side, but loathsome misery—to add to which, a young medical student, who had been sent out on an exploring chemical expedition among a class where his blunders would not be observed, was stealing guiltily down stairs as we crawled slowly up. He had been "practising" on the poor immigrant's wife, beyond a doubt! By-and-by he shall have a diploma for dispatching respectable people behind damask curtains—such are the blessings of scientific attainment.

The sight of that dead mother and weeping father, (for immigrants have hearts,) and of that helpless child, amid this scene of squalor and filth, was enough to make one inquire earnestly why such abuses are permitted by the authorities of a civilized and Christian city. Here are in New York some eighteen hundred or two thousand houses of this description, the keepers of which drive a regular trade, in conjunction with the agents and runners, and wring from the poor immigrant, either in extortionate charges for the occupancy of their wretched dens, or for fraudulent passage-tickets, every cent he brings into the country, and which, properly applied, would have saved him from want and given him abundant time and means to leave the city and obtain employment in the country where it is so much needed. In fact, a very large majority of the immigrants bring money enough with them to pay their way; and few of them would become burdens upon public charity were it not for the rascality of those who lie in wait for them, clutch hold of them the instant they set foot on shore, and never lose sight of them—as long as there is a sixpence in their pockets. Thus three-quarters of the "foreign pauperism" we hear so much about in certain quarters, is the direct consequence of the villany of those who should assist and protect the honest strangers who seek our shores, bringing with them their little store and fully determined to labor honestly for a free and peaceful existence, such as our country practically holds out the promise of to every son and daughter of Adam.

The recent law requiring immigrant agents to be licensed, has produced one good effect—it has reduced the number of those cormorants from seven hundred and over to less than two hundred: and we also believe that those who remain are generally a selection from the best of the class. But after all, any slight melioration to the poor immigrants which may be effected by the reform will most likely be but temporary. As soon as the new state of things gets the hang of the schoolhouse, there will be as much hard-hearted meanness and cold-blooded avarice as ever.

What appears to us to be incontestably the duty of the Municipal Government—or of some government—is first to purify the abominable pest-houses known as "Emigrant Boarding-houses"—compel the landlords to have them well ventilated and regularly cleansed, and supplied with Croton water in every floor—and to absolutely prohibit the sale of ardent spirits or intoxicating drinks of any description on the premises. Next, if such a thing be practicable, there should be public agencies or intelligence offices established, *free*, for the purpose of furnishing farmers in the country, and others, workmen and workwomen from the immigrants. It is a fact, not perhaps generally known or believed, that there is an actual demand at this very moment for thousands of farm-laborers in the vicinity of New York, who would receive comfortable food and good pay for a reasonable amount of labor, which any man can learn in a few hours.

Slice XXIII.—SUNDAY EXCURSIONS, &c.

THERE is a deep philosophy in Sunday Excursions. We need not, perhaps, take the trouble to say that we are not an apologist of a violation of the Sabbath. Any man who disputes the Divine origin of that most beautiful and beneficent institution, must be insane. But the *how* it is best observed—that is the question which we think will bear a great deal more of charitable, liberal discussion than it has ever yet received. Let us consider Sunday in a great City.

There are in the City of New York twenty-five or thirty thousand virtuous young women who live by daily labor, either as domestics or workers with the needle and fingers—seamstresses, cap-makers, book-folders, type-rubbers, fly-girls, &c. &c. In order to earn from two to three dollars and a half a week—which is the range of the wages of the better class, while there are many hundreds who do not receive half as much as the lower sum—they must work from ten to fourteen hours a day, according to their quickness of hand and the hardness of their taskmasters. The domestics must do more than this: they must be up at five o'clock in the morning, and never cease their toil—and that, too, of the hardest kind, such as washing, ironing, cooking, house and chamberwork, nursing, &c. &c.—until ten or eleven at night; and if they should step round the corner during the evening to chat a bit with Paddy, on the sidewalk, there is grumbling enough about it. In addition to these, there are thirty thousand families among the mechanic and laboring classes, each of whose members must work constantly at about the same rate. While the husband is at his shop or under his hod, the wife must do all the cooking, washing, making and mending for the whole family—besides nursing her children and being ready to do a little odd job for a neighbor whenever she can make a shilling by it. There are also about the same number of young men as of young women, employed constantly in their various occupations. From Monday morning to Saturday night these people do nothing but work, work, work. They cannot afford to lose a day nor an hour; for it is only by the strictest economy, and by living in the poorest and cheapest way, that they can make both ends meet on Saturday night and lay by the weekly allowance for the rent, let them do the best they can.

Well—Sunday morning comes, bright and glorious.—The brown-baked City lies gasping and panting for very life beneath the vivid sunshine. Every heart remembers some patch of whispering forest, some glade of gleaming verdure, some brook-divided meadow, through which strayed the feet of happy childhood—or, if born and reared among the brick walls and thickened atmosphere of the City, it has at least dreamed of such little paradise-spots. There is nothing to do, for a whole day—and how natural it is that the first desire of the human being, thus cramped and worn down with work, should be for mere physical relaxation! It could not and would not be otherwise with any class or race of men and women that ever existed. So off they fly, by railroad and ferry-boat and pretty little steamer, or by Yorkville omnibus, or by whatever means of locomotion (even if nothing better than shanks' horses) that they can make accessible. The unmarried people dressed in the Sunday best, pair off in natural divisions; the married, with children tagging behind and crowing baby in father's arms, rush by hundreds to the Harlem cars, which are quickly filled with melancholy looking men, (for your man-animal takes poverty much harder than the women,) wives and mothers rigged out in clean frock and neat straw bonnet, and noisy, crazy children, as happy as General Scott when he took Mexico. We said the car was full—yes, cramming, choking full—and here comes another battalion of pleasure-seekers, scrambling and tumbling over each other to get on board. Jump on—there's plenty of room. Make way there for the ladies—take my seat, madam—ting-a-ling, ding! and off we go—pitching the fat lady who hasn't got her new silk skirt fairly adjusted so as not to wrinkle, headlong into the lap of the gentleman opposite, and setting the tall gentleman who volunteered to stand up—if he could—vibrating between the sides of the car like a patent sort of pendulum. But a general smile goes round the car, in which the sufferers join, and everybody is good-natured—except the fat lady, whose new straw hat, rolled outward at the edges to resemble those abominably expensive and aristocratic Leghorn scoop-shovels which fashionable ladies will wear, as if to mock at the goddess they worship, got smashed at making her *début.* There goes the bell again! and as we live by bread, (and hot rolls,) here is another batch of ardent travellers, panting for the sylvan shades of Westchester. Surely they will be bidden wait for the next car? Not a bit of it! Plenty of room—tumble up—squeeze in—hang on—go ahead—tingle-ing-ling! and so we go!

The three ferries to Hoboken are as busy as salamanders, puffing and blowing and trampling through the hissing waves, all day long beneath the hot and glowing sun—never stopping to rest or feed, save now and then to swallow a hasty wheelbarrow-load of wood, and jog on again. Squadron after squadron of excursioners, men, women, and children, as usual, hurry down in long and unbroken procession, until the brave little ferry-boat, afraid of being sunk with its overload of humanity, gives a little hem! to clear its throat, and leaps away from the wharf.

The Staten Island boats take off, half-hourly, other companies innumerable of expectant people, gasping for a breath of untainted air, and expanding their nostrils with intense delight, as they meet the broad, magnificent breeze from the glorious sea. Coney Island also has its numerous votaries; but they form a species of themselves, and must be dealt with separately.

Under the head of "&c." which you perceive we have cunningly taken on to our title, we will proceed to speak a little of the other excursions, for which New York is famous. The delicious and cheap sail to Greenwood, that most lovely spot of all the lovely environments of New York—the abominable and never-to-be-thought-of-without-going-sick-at-the-stomach expedition to the Fishing Banks, where you are sure to catch a fit of sea-sickness, besides running a reasonable chance of being sun-struck; the free-and-easy voyage to Coney Island, to discover the cause of the clam-disease; the pleasant and wholesome trip to Cedar Grove, Bull's Ferry, Fort Hamilton, (Kingly sea-terrace, fit for Neptune's breezy sister;) to Keyport and Middletown, to glorious New Brighton, and scores of other haunts of coolness and delight, the enumeration of which is not to be thought of at this stage of our lengthening column—what fields for poetical description, for romantic dreaming, for "human" fun! If we must have great cities, crowning the free waves and dictating their path to the white-winged ships that glide over the blue deep's untrampled floor, let them be like our own magnificent New York, surrounded by cool and beautiful retreats, ever open to the weary sons and daughters of Toil—so that in the hot and choking summer, when the hinges of the body grow rusty with heat, and the lungs corrode with dust, they, for their merry sixpence, as well as the nabob with his ostentatious thousands, may hie away and breathe for a while the free air of Heaven, look up far into the depths of a pure blue sky, and hold unconscious communings with the sweet Spirit of the Earth that whispers in the tree-tops—or, more precious still, plunge into the cool ocean and wrestle with the surf, whose very embrace imparts strength and vigor to every limb.

It would not be proper to dismiss the subject of excursions without a passing allusion to some of the disgraceful scenes which are now and then enacted on moonlight and other trips, by rowdies and other improper characters, who come on board without being known in their true character, or who force their way in gangs across the gangway. It is simply a matter of justice to say that neither the managers of the excursions nor the captains of the boats are aware of the character of their troublesome customers, until it is too late, and that they do every thing they can to prevent improper persons from coming on board. It is the imperative duty of the authorities to place a sufficient number of police at the different landings where the boats take on passengers, to preserve strict order, and protect peaceable citizens from the annoyances and insults of those insolent rowdies whose numbers seem to be increasing in New York at a fearful rate, and who grow more audacious as they are less and less frequently punished.

Having thus spoken a good word for the Excursions—which we regard as one of the most agreeable and invaluable advantages of our City—we are afraid that we must proceed to warn respectable citizens, and especially strangers and travellers, that there are certain excursions, moonlight and otherwise, loudly praised in the advertisements, of whose true character they ought to be made aware. And, because we never deal in animosities nor anonymosities, we proceed to say that we allude more particularly to the Coney Island business and the numerous moonlight dancing parties or "flotilla balls." So long as society fails to extinguish prostitution as a profession, and encourages by the patronage and money of its respectable citizens, the cyprians as a class, so long we shall be the last to seek to deprive them of any personal rights and privileges to which others are entitled. But it would seem to be indispensable that the public should know *where* these wretched creatures herd with their cullies and fancy men—so that, if it chooses, the public aforesaid may leave them to themselves, and go, unmolested and uninsulted, about its business. As the political Editors say, when they have said every thing else they can think of—*verbum sap.*

Slice XXIV.—THE THEATRES.

Who has ever read an honest, faithful account of the Theatres of New York—how they are carried on, what they do, and how they do it? Who visits them, who plays in them, and what the influence they are calculated to exert in the community? It is true that we have daily articles, in several papers, about the performances of the night previous, with glowing eulogiums upon each of the performers, upon the author, the manager, the property-man, down to the supernumeraries and the leader of the orchestra. But these articles are either written by a Peter Funk employed and paid by the managers, and inserted at so much a week, more or less, good, bad, or indifferent, or else for the most part are the sublime emanations of some police reporter enamored of the "legitimate" and panting for the honors of a free admission, who thus nobly earns the privilege of a seat in the dress circle when the house is thin, or a *standee* in the lobby on full nights.—As to such a thing as impartial and independent criticism upon Theatres and theatrical performances, in the present state of the relations between editors, reporters, managers, actors,—and actresses—the thing is palpably out of the question. How can you expect a frank and unbiased judgment upon the performance of Mr. George Frederick Cooke Snooks, in the arduous and exciting part of Booby in the "Way to Kick up a Rumpus," when the editor or reporter who is to write it has just been supping on beef-steak and stewed potatoes at Windust's, and regaling himself on brandy and water cold, without, at the expense of the aforesaid George Frederick Cooke Snooks? It is clearly preposterous. To the perceptions of that muddled reporter Mr. Snooks is one of "the most brilliant and promising of our young actors"—is "bound to make a profound sensation in the higher walks of his profession"—and nothing else!

But there *is* such a thing as describing a Theatre in plain and comprehensible language—and we have determined to try our hand at it: so here we are. On the steps we encounter three or four police-officers, as we enter the vestibule, and attempt to pass in. But there are ladies before us, and, you know,

"When a lady 's in the case,
All other things give place."

These are queer-looking ladies, however; and they seem to be entirely alone. They are dressed after a fashion which used to be considered absolutely obscene, but which has come latterly to be extensively imitated in our fashionable and aristocratic drawing-rooms.—They appear to be on intimate terms with the doorkeeper, who gives them a chuck under the chin as they pass through, leaving a strong flavor of bad gin behind them. These are women of the town, utterly abandoned and infamous, who come here as to an open and licensed assignation-house, to prosecute their infernal traffic without fear of molestation—unless they should become too much intoxicated and disturb the peace. *That* is a heinous offence against the laws—but mere public prostitution is not noticed by the law. They come up the same steps and enter at the same door as your wife and daughters—if you have been green enough to bring them to such a place—jostle them in the lobby, and flirt up stairs with a loud laugh and a horrible oath, enough to congeal a young pure heart with horror. This is not the case at the Broadway Theatre. Col. Mann deserves great credit for the reform in this particular. So also we are bound to say of Mr. Niblo, that he never would permit a female to enter his garden unless accompanied by a gentleman.

But let us enter the box. It is a fashionable night, and those "magnificent dancers the Montrejambs" are to perform one of their most beautiful and exciting ballets. The dress-circle is filled with diaphonously-robed ladies, who raise enormous instruments to their eyes—something between a telescope and a pair of goggles is just now "the Cheshire"—the better to examine the lascivious leaps and gyrations of the men and women on the stage; while the men in the pit are by the help of similar contrivances scanning the gazers themselves. Of the exhibitions on the stage it is impossible for us to speak in detail. Although they are witnessed with frantic delight by thousands of virtuous ladies and gentlemen, yet those very

persons would unite in denouncing us as sinners of the deepest dye if we should presume to describe in the morning what they furiously applaud at night.

But Shakspeare—surely you do not condemn Shakspeare? We beg pardon—we had forgot. Shakspeare? yes, we think we have heard of him. Oh yes, now we remember—that is the name of the wooden effigy over the door. He is not to be seen *inside* of the house.—He don't *draw.* The old song is worn out—nothing pays now but new-ditty.

The act is over; and while the poor fellows in the orchestra are scraping their teeth on edge or blowing their brains out in horrible and piercing discord, we will step up stairs. The lobby of the second floor is occupied by a police-officer or two and a dozen newspaper scribblers, reaching over and meekly dodging their heads about among the *paying* spectators, endeavoring to get a peep at the glories of the stage as soon as the curtain shall rise. Their look of mingled effrontery and sheepishness, profundity and maudlin, betrays them at once as members (and in their own opinions no inconsiderable members either) of that great lever of modern times, the Press. You will find their names duly recorded on the free-list at the door. They are constant attendants at the Theatre, and love to write about "crowded and fashionable houses," in a vague sort of idea that thus, for the moment at least, they themselves must have formed a part of said fashionable crowd! Harmless delusion! They stood in the lobby, and never got more than their noses inside of the "house."

But we are at the entrance of the "Saloon"—a large, bare, dreary-looking groggery, with a fattish young woman in a gilt watch-chain and half-mourning at either end, behind a little counter covered with rank-smelling bottles and collapsed doughnuts. Between the acts the room speedily fills with gentlemen who can't wait for their next drink till the play is out, and have left their ladies in the boxes by themselves, to be stared out of countenance by the loafers and libertines in the pit. After a few minutes, guzzling of bad brandy smashers and talking with the simpering bar-maid, the gentlemen return to their patient spouses and delighted daughters, the curtain rises, and the performance goes on.

But the first piece is over, and there is a lull of fifteen or twenty minutes. If you would like to see how much mischief can be done in a quarter of an hour, come with us up stairs. Here you shall see a crowd of painted, drunken women, swearing and blaspheming with every breath, singing snatches of obscene songs, and slapping the men on the shoulder with disgusting familiarity, accompanying the salutation, "Come, ain't you going to treat, old hoss!" In one corner a young man, escaped from his mother's apron-strings, is bargaining with one of these female fiends a bargain which will corrupt his body and deform his very soul to the likeness of hell—which will inevitably lead him on to swindling and fraud, to maintain the polluting and infamous course of life upon which he is now entering, and bring him to the State Prison or an early grave.—Here is a young married man, with a beauteous and blooming wife and a lovely cherub of a baby waiting patiently and confidingly for him at home—the dear, innocent-hearted wife pitying her "poor Henry" who has to stay so late at the store in the business season! How is it possible that he can forget this pure, angelic creature, who would lose her beautiful eyes or her still more beautiful life to save him a single pang, and sit there beside that whited sepulchre, that degraded body without a soul, whose breath smells horribly offensive with rum and drunkenness, and whose only and last desire is to obtain an opportunity under the guise of a coarse caress, to pick his pocket?

Look around this loathsome, reeking chamber, and whom do you see, the companions of these beldames and she-devils? There is a rich banker, yonder a respectable lawyer, here a thriving merchant of spotless credit—on the next bench an artist, beyond him a poet, and mingling with all, a set of rowdy loafers and fire-boys—blacklegs and pickpockets—the scum and sediment of the seething caldron of metropolitan society. From front to rear, from dome to pit, the whole establishment at times is one vast reservoir of immorality, looseness, blasphemy, and obscenity. Moral and virtuous men and women, who visit such a place as this, rarely see the offensive parts which we have described. But we cannot touch pitch without being defiled—nor can one habitually mingle in such a vast scene of promiscuous depravity as this without being more or less contaminated with what he sees and hears.

Slice XXV.—THE OYSTER CELLARS.

The old prejudice against swallowing oysters in Summer, following pretty much every other old prejudice, has been completely exploded by the brilliant success of Decker, Downing, and others, in coaxing the Natives to unnaturalize themselves, and to be ripe and elastic at any season of the year. So we may go boldly down this gaudy cellar, gaping invitingly to receive us, even if it were July, without exciting suspicions that we are after any thing *but* oysters. It is true that as we passed that colored glass door we saw a company of young clerks betting their employers' money with a couple of sharpers at brag, over a bottle of champagne, made in New Jersey and poisoned in New York. But that is no matter. They are fairly on their road to the Penitentiary or the State Prison, and seem to be very much hurried to get to their journey's end. They will scarcely look back to see what becomes of us. If we had worn a jockey cap, a flashy vest, and an extremely short and useless cane, we might perhaps have attracted their attention. On the other side we saw, too, a gentleman and a lady seated in a private stall, discussing a dozen broiled, and iced brandy punch. But they are quite as much absorbed in their own affairs as the young gamblers at cards, and are probably playing for a higher stake—perhaps a husband's honor and a wife's immortal soul. They surely will take no note of us. So let us enter.

But we must have made a mistake. This is surely Aladdin's cave that we have stumbled into. On either hand stretches away, mingling and losing themselves in a gorgeous labyrinth of many-colored glass, damask curtains, and shaded lights, a long row of mirrored arcades, festooned with costly blue and crimson silk and wreathed with golden carved work, the interior lined with plate glass, furnished with a luxurious divan of the latest

spring pattern, and the walls adorned with exquisite and voluptuous drawings—now a woodcock that might have ruffled the easel of Landseer, and now a half-clad woman who might have glowed beneath the pencil of Brochart. Between these epicurean riches stretches a broad aisle magnificently carpeted, and hung with splendid chandeliers, half shaded with ground glass, and streaming a mysterious gleam, half bright, half shadow, through the apartment. In front of the little recess, where we have taken our seats, rises a graceful and fairy structure, of lightly-carved wood, painted cream-white, and incrusted with arabesque designs in gilt—the whole surmounted with a rich slab of jasper-veined marble, wrought with mirror-like polish. In silver stands, carelessly distributed about this beautiful marble table, are crystal decanters, richly cut into classic forms, and costly silver pitchers, of delicate shape and exquisite workmanship. In these decanters lie coiled up the venomous serpents that have stung the life of so many hundred thousand noble hearts, corrupted such myriads of pure souls to the capacity and similitude of demons—beggared so many wives and daughters—made desolate so many homes and hearths—and spread desolation and despair through all ranks of society. Taste, drink, riot, grow mad, and die! 'Tis only sixpence a glass! Cheap enough—yet oh, rash tippler, only to be purchased at last with the life of thy immortal soul. In those dainty decanters, smiling amber-hued and rosy—flashing the spiced air with purple beams and glowing with golden and fiery essence—lie the spells that once conjured to the lip, will lead thee to ruin, madness, blear-eyed idiocy, and untimely death. Dare and die!

We have described here only a "first-class" cellar—of which there are not more than half a dozen in all the metropolis. They grow gradually dimmer and more real, as they increase in number—dropping, one after another their gaudy and masking finery, until we approach the dingy, noisome three-cent cellar on the Five Points, with its rotten, break-neck ladder-stairs, its single foul-smelling light, its reeking and smoke-covered walls—its vile and poisoned brandy—and its group of half-naked white and negro men and women dancing in the middle of the floor, or piled indiscriminately into the verminous bunks that line the walls. The road from first to last is plain and straight-forward, and descended by easy and almost imperceptible gradations. First, the dashing young man, his pockets well filled with money, rigged out in the "ridiculous excess" of fashion, makes his appearance in the gorgeous underground saloon frequented by none but aristocratic rowdies and upper-crust blacklegs. Here he soon forms what he considers some "elegant associations," in a set of veteran libertines, debauchees, and gamblers, who initiate him speedily into all the higher and more seductive mysteries of dissipation. From the splendid cellar they adjourn to the aristocratic and well-furnished gambling-house, where every thing is conducted with the best-bred quietness and deliberation, and where splendidly-dressed women flit mysteriously about in lascivious gestures, glancing swiftly through a doorway, and then disappearing as if by enchantment—leaving, however, the fire of lustrous, passionful eyes burning in the breast of the young neophyte—fire that will burn forevermore, and which will lead him gradually, yet swiftly, to a brief dream of fierce and guilty pleasure—then to ruin and abandonment—and then to crime, drunkenness, or suicide—perhaps all three in turn.

From the gambling-house to the brothel is so easy, so brief a distance, that few there are who do not take it. This soon reduces the purse, saps the constitution, increases the appetite for drink; and in a few months the dashing blood becomes the feeble, maudlin sot, and drops rapidly from one haunt and degree of dissipation to another, until he finds himself—or the policeman finds him—a filthy, ragged, idiotic vagabond, herding with negroes and low sidewalkers in the holes and corners of the City, and ends his miserable career with a death that comes as the only blessing yet left for him on earth.

We should not be doing justice to our description of the bar-rooms of New York, if we were to overlook the numerous second-story coffee-houses, which have become fashionable resorts of dissipation within a year or two. These man-traps, besides the usual variety of liquor and cigars, are baited with a good-looking female barkeeper, who dispenses smiles and smashers, and mixes you a piquant jest in your julep,—all for a shilling. In these places, as soon as evening sets in, scores of young bloods and would-be dandies gather, drinking liquor which they do not like, and smoking cigars which make them sick, for the privilege of hanging about the counter, and exchanging a word or a smile now and then with the divinity behind. From the reeking theatres, the smoky billiard-rooms, and slippery bowling-alleys, midnight brings crowds of customers of every variety, from the accomplished swindler to the merest ambitious tyro who has robbed his master's till to cut a swell among folks, who talk balderdash, and soak their miserable brains with brandy till they are ready for any enterprise of infamy, and sally out staggering up the street, to tumble senseless and swine-like into the first hole that opens to receive them. These bar-rooms, besides the positive and active influences they exert in brutalizing and debasing the minds of young men, are the accredited seminaries of every species of vice—the half-way houses between the first glass and the gutter, the theatre and the brothel. Hidden from the public gaze by closed window-shutters, and removed from the *bruit* of the street, they offer an inviting resting-place where young men not yet quite corrupted are furnished with every facility for stultifying their intellects, brutalizing their tastes, and inflaming their appetites. They are the most dangerous because the least ostentatious of pest-houses; and the young man who commences by being enticed into them, is pretty sure to finish his career in infamy and crime.

These establishments, and hundreds—we might say thousands—of similar ones of all grades and qualities of evil, are well known to the police, and could easily be suppressed by the authorities. *Why* they are not, perhaps you would not like us to be committed for contempt of court for explaining. When the citizens take it into their heads to elect men to office who are above the reach of interest in the exercise of their duties, our laws will be found amply sufficient to suppress these powerful temptations to dissipation, and rescue thousands upon thousands of the weak-minded and amiable from courses which are now leading them irresistibly to infamy and ruin.

Slice XXVI.—SUNDAY IN NEW YORK.

A strong man in action stopping to take breath—a racehorse panting between the heats—a ship pausing ere it plunges headlong down the mountain of the storm, and leaps on her course—are faint figures to indicate the abrupt and absolute repose that overtakes the metropolis every seventh day. In other places the contrast between Sunday and weekday is not so striking—for, although the quiet may be as complete, yet the noise and tumult are not so great, and the effect of the contrast, which here absolutely startles one, is wanting. If one fall asleep on a railroad, the stopping of the cars will be pretty sure to wake him; so the New Yorker becomes so accustomed to the ceaseless, the incredible din of Broadway—into whose rushing river-bath of dust and clamor every one dips at least twice a day—that the sudden, solemn, absolute silence of the Sabbath comes upon him like a sweet shock, rousing into activity his higher and more contemplative faculties, and laying, for a time, the fierce and remorseless spirit of Business that during all the week has been dragging him about by the hair.

In the narrow streets and alleys down-town, where usually the rattle of drays drowns out consciousness itself from your brain, and the sidewalks are piled hill-high with boxes, bales, and bundles, now the footfall echoes and re-echoes loudly on the smooth-worn flag, and the long lines of lofty warehouses extend with the prospect unbroken by drays or merchandise. In Wall-street, late so fiercely crowded, and struggling each man as if for life, all is still as death or the desert. The Dog-man has disappeared from the Custom-house steps—the doomed Canary birds no longer draw up their miniature wheelbarrows of seeds—the Shaving Cream man has smoothed himself out of sight—the innumerable shaving-shops down cellar have closed their cavernous jaws—and the Rotunda is as empty as Judge ——'s hat when his head is in it. The whole lower part of the City, where usually one would think, from the noise and hubbub, that the continent was running through a funnel, and this was the spout, is now as silent and lonely as a city of the olden time deserted centuries ago by its inhabitants, and left to the winds and sands of the desert.

But in Broadway the Sabbath contrast is perhaps even greater than in the great marts of trade and commerce. The pavement is as still as if an omnibus had never rattled over it, and the bewildered sunshine goes stumbling along trying to find some accustomed plate-glass window through which to look in upon pretty goods and prettier ladies. Before the palace-stores of fashion no liveried carriages are waiting, and on the walk nothing is seen but the unbent shadows of the lamp-posts. The roar and crash of the omnibuses is hushed, and the dust lies unsprinkled by the inevitable watering-pot on wheels, or whirls away in little suffocating eddies, whither and where it will. The Large Roasted Italian Chesnut Man has taken in his warming-pan and furnace, and the little girls who sell fancy windmills on Stewart's steps are, we hope, at Sunday-School learning their lessons.

In Chatham-street and the Bowery there is a little more life, but the change is still very great and gratifying, as an unmistakable evidence of the general regard in which Sunday is held by all classes of our population. There are, we know, a few loafers and rowdies who gather about the Five Points and the Hook, on the wharves, and in the grog-cellars of the by-streets, who neither know nor care whether it is Sunday or not. But they are not apparent. Their haunts are for the most part underground, and they do not mar the general serenity of a New York Sabbath. In the Bowery and Chatham-street, too, the absence of the omnibuses is very grateful; and we are sincerely sorry to hear that efforts are making to get some of the lines, both in Broadway and the Bowery, to run on Sunday. We trust that there is, if not real morality, at least regard enough for the physical welfare of mankind, among our citizens to promptly frown down any such attempts as these. The omnibus proprietors themselves, we are sure, do not wish to run their vehicles on the Sabbath; for the increased wear and tear of carriages, waste of horse-flesh, &c., would more than overbalance the gains. Besides, it would be cruel and oppressive in no slight degree to compel the worthy and some of them Christian men now engaged in omnibus driving to either run on Sunday or lose their situations. They are most of them men of families, and their wives find it no easy matter to get along with the six dollars a week which their husbands earn: but if they were to work *every* day they would soon break down or die, and thus leave their families destitute. The seventh day of rest is an indispensable necessity of all laboring men—and especially those so constantly employed, and in all sorts of weathers, as the omnibus-driver. Let the Sabbath ever be sacred to rest.

If Broadway is the great artery of New York, through which all the blood and bloods of town must course, Nassau-street and its environments may be called its brain, pulsating ever with the beating of a printing-engine, and throwing off innumerable nerves, in the shape of newsboys, to the rest of the system. But on Sunday even this is still. It is true that the *Sun* and *Herald*, and perhaps some other papers, issue extras when a steamer arrives on Sunday, even if there be not an item of news, and they are frequently cried in the very front of the churches during divine service. We of *The Tribune* never do this, and our office is never open on Sunday. Early every Sabbath morning, too, the voices of Sunday-paper newsboys are loud and incessant for two or three hours. Most of the newspaper offices, however, are, like *The Tribune*, closed on the Sabbath; and we believe that public opinion will eventually compel all others to follow the example. Indeed, this public opinion is rapidly becoming aware of the great fact that the Sabbath is a physical as well as spiritual necessity to the world, and that, were it not for its blessed intervals of rest and recuperation, thousands of persons whose occupations are uncommonly arduous or exhausting would either die or become insane before the prime of their years. The united and unequivocal testimony of physicians, physiologists, philosophers, magistrates, and legislators, has been so widely diffused over the world by the benevolent labors of the American Tract Society and other religious institutions, that all classes of the community are becoming familiar with them. And should these lines fall into the hands of any man, woman, or child who has not yet become convinced that life and health are deeply interested in observing the Sabbath, we would earnestly advise him or her to go to the American Tract Society's office, 150 Nassau-street, and procure "The Sabbath Manual," by Rev. Justin Edwards—one of the most perspicuous, complete, and eloquent works on the Sabbath we have ever read. They will also find peculiarly interesting, in relation to this subject, tracts 8, 20, 116, 163, 334, 336, 415, 474, and 502.

But to return to New York on Sunday. If from what we have said, you conclude that signs of life and animation are wanting throughout the Sabbath, you are greatly mistaken. We spoke of the middle of the day. But in the morning at nine o'clock, punctual as an eclipse of the moon or a man to whom you have promised money, the Sunday-School bells begin to ring from a thousand steeples—and, despite the ill-natured remarks of people who are ashamed of themselves for hating the Sabbath and its institutions, we always find it most delightful music—with more heart and soul and meaning in it than all the *caterwaulini* to which the walls of the Tabernacle have ever resounded.

Then, like troops of fairies summoned by the sound of a familiar bell, bright-faced children in their fresh and pretty Sunday gowns and jackets, swarm the streets, and take their way to Sunday-School—a place whose charm it is difficult to describe, but most beautiful to acknowledge and feel. Never in all our wide experience among children—and we have known and loved thousands of them—have we found a boy or girl accustomed to attend Sunday-School, who did not feel it a pleasure to go there, and a real misfortune to be compelled, by any unforeseen event, to stay away. Through rain and sunshine, in Summer and Winter, off they go, as happy as young lambs, and also as innocent and as beautiful—for all children are beautiful.

In another hour and a half comes church—and then, if you would see how many people New York out-of-doors *can* hold, just look out, or join the crowd, and observe, as you are gently urged along by the force of the current into which you have dropped. Such a procession of beautiful ladies and attentive cavaliers cannot be seen elsewhere nor at any other time. There, too, the staid matron leaning upon the arm of her gray-headed but still stalwart husband, as they march proudly in front of their children and grandchildren, form picturesque and pleasing groups; while here and there some fond couple, still lingering within the enchanted atmosphere of the honeymoon, move stealthily along, their faces beaming with happiness. And how different the aspect and bearing of the throng from the rude crowds that rush and jostle each other on the walk in weekdays! Surely it is a blessed thing that the calm, love-inspiring Sabbath comes once a week to reunite the scattered family, and gather up the broken links of domestic affection, that sweetest and most blessed tie of earth. It is difficult not to believe that, without the Sabbath, society would inevitably retrograde to barbarism.

As soon as evening sets in, the City undergoes a change sudden and great as magic. Broadway, which all day save church-hours has been so lonely and deserted, now swarms with a dense crowd of men and women who do not, through the week, find leisure for a promenade. The great bulk of them are servant-girls, with their beaux and brothers, lovers and friends, who wait eagerly through the whole week for the setting of the Sabbath sun, that they may rush into the streets, and for a few hours enjoy the luxury of being free to do as they please. The bookfolders, the seamstresses, the fly-girls, the type-rubbers, the straw-braiders,—all the working girls from all parts of the City and every occupation,—have also found their sweethearts, and are out for a promenade in Broadway. They look fresher and walk more eagerly, and with far more energy and *aplomb* than the weekday loungers and idlers in our fashionable thoroughfare; and every face wears an expression of determination to make the most of the brief hour of recreation which is permitted to all classes. The sidewalk gives out new echoes—unaccustomed dialects break their necks against the unheeding window-shutters of the closed shops, and Broadway is no longer but a continuation, a suburb, of the Bowery. Far into the night thousands of footsteps patter upon the pavement, and the hum of mingling voices comes over the ledge of our far-up window like the music of the distant surf. At length, one by one, the few lights along the street disappear—the noise of falling feet grows more and more interrupted—conversation and strange bursts of laughter come less frequently and then cease entirely—the moonlight streams cold and glistening across the flag-stones—midnight sounds echoingly from steeple to steeple—and Sunday in New York is over.

Slice XXVII.—BEHIND THE SCENES.

Our previous article on Theatres did not go behind the scenes, nor did it contain but a passing allusion to what was enacting upon the stage for the elevation and refinement of the public—or, as it is expressed on the drop-curtain,

"To raise the genius, and to mend the heart."

We now propose to penetrate a little farther into the mysteries of the stage and the Green-Room, and see the practical effects of the drama, as exhibited in the lives, character, and associations of those engaged in this moral and ennobling profession. In doing this we utterly disclaim any intention of indulging in the remotest personality. Combining the results of personal knowledge and observation, extended over a number of years, and in theatrical establishments of various grades, we shall speak only in general terms of general evils. If our remarks offend those who are engaged in the theatrical profession, it will be simply because they are true. We wish to say also, that there are of course many exceptions to the picture we draw, and draw from life. We know many noble men and women whose great strength of character and purity of heart have enabled them to pass unscathed through the ordeal of the stage, and upon whose name calumny has never breathed. It will be enough to mention Macready, our own Forrest, Mrs. Charles Kean, Mrs. Mason, to remind the reader that the stage has not yet lost all grace, and to inspire a hope in its ultimate purification and restoration as a conservator of public morals and one of the most vivid exponents of poetry and exalted passion. Many names of less renown also occur to us, both of men and women, whose possessors would adorn any walk of life, and are as pure as their intellects are cultivated; but a partial catalogue would only be injustice to those who should be omitted, and a complete one is of course impracticable. We paint classes, and institutions as they appear in the general; and the very exceptions to what we shall have to say of the dramatic profession, are those who will best know and feel its general truth.

In the first place let us stop to deny, in the most unqualified terms, the morality of the lessons generally inculcated by the stage. So far from this a very great majority of all the standard plays and farces on the stage depend mostly for their piquancy and their power of interesting an audience, upon intrigues with married women, elopements, seductions, bribery, cheating, and fraud of every description—set off with a liberal allowance of *double entendre,* broad indecency, (which the license of the performer generally converts into positive obscenity,) and a general prevalence of profanity better becoming the inmates of a prison or groggery than ladies and gentlemen. Stage costume, too, whenever there is half a chance, is usually made as immodest and lascivious as possible; and a freedom and impropriety of demeanor prevails among the characters of the piece, which would be kicked out of private society, the instant it should have the audacity to make its appearance there. In a word, the whole end, aim, and effort of a great majority of plays, farces, and ballets presented on the stage is to excite the animal passions and gratify the lowest and most depraved of human tastes. It is true that now and then a small chunk of sentiment or patriotism or philanthropy is thrown in awkwardly among the crudities and immoralities of the scene—but it evidently has no business there, and hastens to get its little round of applause and get itself forgotten as soon as possible. At many of the smaller theatres things have been carried to an outrageous pass—until the stage became little better than a brothel turned inside out, and the whole character of the performances was so baldly filthy and indecent as to be absolutely safe from description. We appeal to the respectable married gentlemen Above Bleecker, whom we often see poking slyly about the Olympic and Chatham, to answer us candidly, Would you, on any consideration, take your wives and daughters to these places, or have them exactly aware of what you see and hear there—ay, and *do* there?

But it is behind the scenes that the beauties of the drama (we don't mean the supernumeraries and ballet-girls) are to be seen. The great star of the evening, whose fame fills the columns of several enlightened and impartial journals at twenty dollars a week, has perhaps a wife and half a dozen children in Europe, while in this country (having but recently arrived) he has but a wife and one child. He will improve, however, as he goes on; and if, before the year is out, he have not a wife in every principal city in the Union, it will not be because the code of the drama has any objection to interpose to such an arrangement, nor because the fastidious Public, who faints at sight of a piano without pantalettes, is at all concerned about the morals of its favorite. These plain statements will doubtless be howled at by many members of the profession, as well as their toadies and hangers-on, whose only happy moments are when they are eating or drinking with an actor, trying to catch the eye of an acquaintance on the stage while the play is going on, or making love to a stout-armed actress, who says "I seen you in the second tier," and whose face is trowelled over with chalk mortar, tipped off with a vermilion rose in the middle of each cheek. But it was absolutely requisite to our plan to make these disagreeable disclosures. It is only by its effect upon those engaged in it that we can judge whether any occupation is wholesome or not; and having undertaken to dissect New York, slice by slice—as the old fogies used to demonstrate the human brain—how could we justify ourselves to our own conscience if we were to gloss over and whitewash things as we went along? We assert, then, that it is very rarely that a woman can connect herself for life with the theatrical profession and maintain her reputation—even whether she deserves it or not; and this is the most conclusive evidence of the foul and noxious moral atmosphere that surrounds the stage.

One of the most noteworthy things one sees behind the scenes in some theatrical establishments, is the number of elderly, gray-headed, and dilapidated old codgers watching at the side-wings, exploring up and down the dark vistas that flank the stage, breaking their shins over the attributes of the carpenter and property-man, and hanging about the Green-Room, looking wistfully in to that greedily-coveted paradise. These gentlemen are "patrons of the drama!" They like to have their names appear conspicuously in complimentary benefit arrangements, while they themselves love to be seen behind the scenes, bowing to kings with pasteboard crowns and a pine stick wrapped in foolscap for a sceptre; and absolutely trembling with happiness at a smile from a countess in calico, or a squeeze of the hand from a fairy of ten stone in pink legs and book muslin. What such ridiculous old animals live for, we have never been able satisfactorily to determine; although, doubtless, like monkeys and small-potato politicians, they have their appointed end.

The Green-Room is a place respecting which the most erroneous and exaggerated ideas have been formed. It is simply a large, barnish-looking room, generally painted yellow, (the green is in those who have a hankering after it,) meanly and scantily furnished with seats, and a large board hung against the wall, covered with innumerable bits of wafery paper, the top one of which contains the *cast* of the performance. The only ornamental article in the room (saving the ladies' presence) is a large swing mirror, in which the female performers practise their attitudes and see whether their skirts are disposed with an eloquence calculated to captivate the hearts of the spectators. To this room, actors and actresses resort during the intervals in which they are not wanted on the stage. Some look over their parts, endeavoring to retain a line or two of the author as they rush upon the stage. Some dispute about the relative merits of this or that actor, where Mrs. So-and-so made her first appearance, or where she was playing in such-and-such a year. This, repeated over and over again every night in the year, forms the staple of the conversation and incident of the Green-Room.

Such is a fair and candid picture of the characters and carryings-on in many of our popular theatres.—Such members of the company as do not come under the delineations we have made, keep themselves aloof from their fellow professionals, remain in their own dressing-rooms, and only leave them when it is necessary to make their appearance on the stage. They are almost universally hated, ridiculed, and despised by the rest of the company.

It gives us sincere pleasure to conclude this sketch by stating that in the new establishments, the Broadway Theatre, and the Astor-place Opera-House—as well as the pretty little *bijou* box of Mr. Burton in Chambers-street—we think we perceive unmistakable indications of an improving state of things in the drama, corresponding to the higher and purer moral requirements of the age. We trust that the new manager of the old Park Theatre will also have the courage, as he unquestionably has the energy, to wrest that establishment from the disgrace which attaches to too many theatres, and to place it upon a better and firmer footing than it ever attained even in its most prosperous days. Let the rule be imperative—banish utterly every facility for grog-drinking within the walls of the theatre, and admit no woman unaccompanied by a gentleman. These simple reforms would do much to rescue the stage, by improving the character of the audience, and would be the hopeful forerunner of still better things.

Slice XXVIII.—THE NEWSBOYS.

The Newsboy is a result of the modern civilization. Greece and Rome, nor yet Egypt, whence came to all the world Letters, Mathematics, and Mummies, with all their boasts—and they were fond enough of boasting—could not brag of the Newsboy. Of King Cheops much has been said that has been forgotten! and all that is positively known respecting him is that he lived and died and left a great three-cornered pile of rocks behind, or rather above him. But of King Mark McGuire, the Sovereign of the Newsboys, we know something much better than pyramids. He is a Prince who exacts the most implicit obedience from his turbulent subjects, and whose royal labors are exclusively confined to the enlightenment of the world. Whenever a vessel arrives with intelligence from the realms of his sister sovereign Victoria, or that wilful, capricious Republic of France, His Majesty the King of Nassau-street, attended by his Prime Minister, Tommy Ryan; his Secretary of State, Greek; and all the under Officers of the Court, comes forth in state; while the whole community are in the utmost excitement respecting their movements.

The genuine Newsboy, in his full development and activity, does not exist, except in New York. Your Philadelphia Newsboy, now, has a sort of slow-and-easy, deliberate sing-song, which inspires you with any thing but a desire to read the news. But in New York, the quick, snapping cry, uttered while under a full run, and trailing along like the smoke of a steam-pipe with the boat at the top of her speed, communicates a sort of excitement to the dullest laggard in the street, and sets the whole city in a state of effervescence directly. The Newsboy is the pearlash dropped into the sour cider of everyday life, making it hiss and bubble with an importance not its own. Without him, the Archimedean lever, the Press, would lose much of its power and half its activity. He is the antennæ which feel, and forewarn the community of approaching news—the taster of the great cup of Newspaperism, which everybody quaffs. Formerly the Newsboy cried the leading features of his news—but he found that many hundreds did not care to hear any more, and passed on without buying. So now he has become chary of his crying, and gives as little as possible of the purport of his budget. If you stop him and inquire what is the news, you *may* get a civil answer—but we would advise you not to rely too much on the accuracy of the intelligence. If you would have the news, fork over your pennies for an *Extra Tribune,* and then read it honestly, and with a clear conscience.

We have never made the attempt to count the Newsboys, but, we suppose, from a general observation of them in all their haunts and localities, that there are about three hundred regularly and permanently on duty—increased by fifty or more on extraordinary occasions. When the first Newsboy appeared, or where he came from, no man has yet told: we suppose, as to his parentage, he was the son of an Oysterman, from whom he derived his voice, and the free and self-possessed manner with which he employs it in the street.

In his dress, he does not affect the latest fashions.—No Newsboy, no legitimate Newsboy, has ever been seen in a whole suit. The uniform of his Craft is a slouched cloth cap, dilapidated roundabout and breeches, no shoes or stockings, and a dirty face with hands to match.

Notwithstanding the diligent and elaborate search we have instituted, we have not been able to ascertain where the Newsboy has furnished himself with his dress. We have inquired at all the Tailors: Not one of them is Tailor to the Newsboys. At the slop-shops they work for the Sailors, not for the Newsboys. At the second-hand Clothes-Dealers in Chatham-street, they do not recollect to have ever had a Newsboy for a customer. Some have supposed their rigs, or fit-outs, are thrown into the street over night, by unseen hands, and picked up early in the morning by the Boys. Others, that they grow upon the Newsboys by degrees, like moss about tree-trunks; that one day a pair of trousers comes, the next week what they call a coat, and then, as the season advances, an old cloth cap. For ourselves, we believe these suits have descended to the 19th Century from a remote antiquity; that they are fragments of the costume of a remote period, artfully reconstructed; and it is not impossible (and the heathen manner in which they are freely riddled gives plausibility to the conjecture) that some of them have figured in the Crusades. Find us the Tailor who makes the Newsboy's Uniform, and we will tell you when the American Union is going to be dissolved.

We are afraid Tom Newsboy is a trifle profligate; he swears, we know, freely; drinks, fights, and very often stays out all night. This last we must not dwell on too strongly as a vice, for it is often a necessity. Tom having no home to go to, and not thinking it worth while to be at a charge for lodgings, takes up his quarters for the night in a box or bunk, under a stoop or in an entryway, where half a dozen of them frequently huddle together, heads and points, with a shaggy dog in their midst, as good a fellow as any of them.

Tom indulges too in games of Chance, and is scarcely ever without dice, small cards, and other implements of hazard in his pocket. We believe he has some games peculiar to himself, of his own devising. He pitches pennies sometimes, like other boys, or plays at marbles; but this he holds to be a small business. In general he disdains the common sports of youth, and rises on the wing into a loftier region of its own.

The most extraordinary feature, perhaps, in the whole history of the Newsboy, is his profound passion for the Theatre. This is one of the earliest uses to which he devotes his first earnings. The Chatham or the Olympic has, always, the first-fruits. At the very opening of the doors he throws himself into the pit, and with judicial steadiness watches the progress of the piece. He generally takes possession of the middle of the benches: many of them, by inscribing their names thereupon with a knife, securing them against invasion, and occupying them (as they suppose) by as good a right, and with more regularity nightly, than the rich frequenters of Grace Church and St. Patrick's, their pews, with their names emblazoned on polished plates, at an annual rent of five hundred dollars the pew.

He affects (in his dramas) thunder and lightning, long-swords, casques, and black-whiskered villains, with mysterious exits and entrances, in preference to everyday life. In bloody and violent death-scenet he revels like a little Pirate. There was a Mr. Kirby—he is gone now, poor fellow—we hope he passed into the other world at the R. H. door!—who had great favor among the Newsboys, by his convulsive and awful manner of yielding up the ghost on the Stage. Many boys, whose engagements did not permit an entire attendance, have paid the full price to be in at one of Kirby's death-struggles. They were unquestionably the most magnificent things (of their kind) ever seen in this country. The Newsboys, however, held the late Mr. Kirby to a strict account. If he omitted a single groan or distortion of feature, there was a general howl of disapprobation through the Pit, and that Actor was compelled, more than once, to go through the death-struggle a second and even a third time, till it satisfied the high requirements of these young censors.

Not only in his keen judgment in such questions of Art, but in all Newsboy accomplishments, the New York practitioner, compared with the Newsboys of other Cities, takes the lead by several lengths: in speed of foot, power of vociferation, rapidity of utterance, force of character—in fact, like every thing New York, he is at the head of his class. After the Theatre, the chief luxury of the Newsboy is, in common, a glass or half a dozen glasses of a crimson-whity mixture, supposed to be or to stand for ice-cream; and, in winter, an equal number of cups of gloomy coffee, at a penny a cup, as the other is a penny a glass. No wonder they have customs and usages of their own; for this is, certainly, a peculiar business, which summons forth young boys, mere lads, at all hours, associating them in a manner with the mighty Press, at that early time of life, and cramming their pockets with silver, more spending-money than the richest merchant's son, which they may disburse, when, how, and where they desire, without accountability to any one. They often make two and three dollars from a Steamer's "Extra," in an hour; selling from fifty to one hundred and fifty papers, at a heavy advance on first cost. It is the duty of the Newsboy to watch the Press, as a cat watches a mouse; to be on hand at all hours, seasonable and unseasonable, for foreign or domestic news of importance, as much as the Editor or Proprietor of the Journal. At the moment of delivery, he seizes the reeking paper, and rushing forth like one distracted, they fill all the streets of the city, far and near, in an inconceivably short space of time, with their bold and startling cries.—These are not always to be taken as Gospel. They sometimes bring on a Revolution impromptu, and depose a King without notice. Against certain members of the Royal Families of Europe, they seem to cherish a bitter spite. We believe the Newsboys itched for months to announce the deposition or abdication of Louis Philippe: As much might have been inferred from the fervor—the more than fervor, the fury—with which they bellowed out his downfall when (at last) it did come. We think, as a body, they would announce the flight of Prince Albert and Queen Victoria, and the disruption of the British Empire, with the greatest satisfaction. As in all communities there are leaders, so there are Chief Newsboys, or Foremen; small Capitalists, who furnish the papers to the boys, requiring an account at night, and allowing them a part of the profits, or reasonable wages. It is to these, of whom King Mark McGuire is the Chief, that the "bursted-up" boys apply, to be set up again in business, when by improvidence or neglect, they have become insolvent.—The Newsboys, for the sake of the fresh air, sometimes make short trips down East, or to Albany, in the Steamboats, or on the Cars between the Cities, getting a free passage (with a Newspaper or two to the Clerk or Conductor) and selling what they can by the way. The City is, however, their main-stay.

We have been told that Newsboys have been seen at Cock-fights, in back-yards and subterranean places about the City; and that they have even figured as owners of Game-fowls. This we do not believe. It's a scandal put in circulation by the enemies of the brotherhood. That they swear, fight, cheat, and run wild at night, we have frankly admitted, but the Cock-fights we deny. We have a friendship for the Order, and we must make a stand somewhere. It has also been asserted (from some touches of grandeur we have noticed glimmering out from among his rags—we can believe this) that in the pride of his spirit, and in the dignity of his intimate connection with the Public Journals, two or three Newsboys have been known to club together and purchase, at auction, a horse and wagon—both of light build—(value of the outfit, including harness, tail-board, &c., $4.25) with which they have been seen sporting in afternoon rides on the Avenue, like so many young gentlemen of fortune. We wonder whether it has ever occurred to any Newsboy of reflecting turn, what a mighty instrument for good or evil, he has in that voice of his—the peace of how many families he has broken or cheered by his loud and long cry of Steamer or Packet—what mischief he has wrought by false alarms—how many ears have been strained to catch its far-off sound, whose all of weal or wo in this life, hung suspended on the Newsboy's breath.

A piece of advice we shall venture, as the friends of these young gentlemen: If the passion is strong upon them to dabble in Literature, let them stick to the legitimate business of the Morning and Evening Newspapers, regular and extra, and not allow themselves to be seduced by grown men (who should have more sense and more self-respect) to deal in dirty French Novels, and filthy Compositions of home manufacture, on a similar model. Let them shun the contraband sale of obscene books and prints, as they would red-hot coals of fire; which would burn up in them every good principle, and reduce them to a sapless, ashy, and worthless old age. We can imagine no more pitiful or revolting sight than one of these children, under the promptings of some old fiend in mischief from behind his "respectable" counter, sneaking about the Hotels, Steamboat Landings, and Public Parks, having concealed in his bosom the seeds of ruin, and stealthily seeking to cast them in the laps of others. God must weep and devils grin, when poison is so diffused with a double damnation, killing the soul of seller and buyer with a subtle and fatal power. Boys! you had better jump into a Furnace at white-heat, than to have any thing more to do with this low and nasty traffic! Stick to the Newspapers!

What kind of citizens these Newsboys will make—what kind of creatures will spring from these mixed elements of turmoil, street-running, precocious activity of body and mind, and precocious profusion of cash, no one can guess; for the system—started some ten years since—has not been long enough in operation to bring any of them of age. Our best wishes are with the Boys.

Slice XXIX.—THE PATENT MEDICINE MEN.

We approach this subject with a slight qualm of conscience—to say nothing of the stomach—ignorant of what sort of pill may be our potion for daring to meddle with these liberal prescriptionists of the constitution, nor how they will "take" the dose we are putting up for them.

It is quite customary to laugh at the Patent Medicine Men—but on the principle that they laugh best who laugh last, we think the Doctors, as usual, have quite the best end of the bargain. Of course, in treating of the Patent Medicine makers, we have no intention of going into the "regulars"—although if the truth were known we doubt not that their saddlebags and vials would be found to contain quite as many nostrums as the big-labelled bottles of our "patent" friends. After all, and admitting that this business has a good deal of quackery in it, yet there must be some virtues in many of the remedies, or they never could have reached such immense popularity among all classes of the community, high and low, rich and poor, old and young, learned and ignorant, as they have done. Indeed, if the veritable Tribune Slicer himself were compelled to choose between the "regular" and the "patent" practices—which the God of Health mercifully forbid!—he would be sorely puzzled for a decision. It would be something like having to decide between hanging and drowning.

Altogether, it would seem that the Patent Medicine business is as respectable and as profitable as any other occupation and calling, and probably doesn't do any more harm, at the worst, than the "regular" profession. We have only to say to our readers, that, in purchasing their Patent Medicines, they should remember that all is not gold that shines, and that those who make the most noise have very often the least merit.

The Patent Medicine business is much overdone, even to an extent beyond almost any other. A few having realized a fortune, hundreds—thousands have rushed into it and lost the little means they expected would so rapidly accumulate. It is an uncommonly flattering business considering *alone* the actual cost of the stock; hence thousands have been rashly invested in the manufacture and distribution of remedies without counting the tremendous cost of popularity: and it is obvious, that unless large sales are made, ruin will follow; so that, by a safe calculation, it is believed ninety in every hundred fail, who undertake the business.

The manner of doing this remarkable business is invariably to manufacture large quantities, and establish agencies in every part of the country; it being almost without exception a commission business, and this the only means of extending it. Of course, without a very large capital, nothing of late years can be done to compete with the already established remedies.

Townshend labored two years and accomplished nothing. Finally, Mr. Clapp, of Albany, who is wealthy, joined him, investing ample means, since which the Sarsaparilla era soon reached its zenith. But as every thing must have its day, it is rapidly declining.

Many have been deluded into the belief that to "come out largely" would bring customers from the four parts of the country, and have soon run out every dollar paying advertisements; then they fill the papers with "wants" like this;—"Wanted—one thousand dollars, with a partner to engage in a business in which $5000 can be made in a month," &c., &c.

Despairing of ever obtaining a livelihood by such precarious means, they either go to work at something useful, or engage in a more desperate effort to humbug the sick.

Nor is it now a simple matter to introduce a new curative, as besides the various popular nostrums, hundreds of respectable physicians in all parts of the country, (and small druggists,) seeing such a demand for Patent Medicines, and knowing that if they did not, others would, sell, have made up "cure-alls," and distributed them in their vicinity; but as they do not understand the business, and have but little capital, half of them resume their legitimate profession.

When Dr. Brandreth began, a medicine could more easily work its way to fame with less means, as competition was not so strong as to keep it back; but even then without skill none could succeed.

As a body there is equal talent engaged in this business to any other. It is noticed that medicines which are the most extensively advertised by fulsome laudations, as rapidly decline, as they go up; the proprietors thinking if they make money at all they will do it soon. Others, who have confidence in the intrinsic value of their remedies, pursue a different course, fearing that great excitement and exaggeration will impair the confidence of the public, and shorten their popularity. With ability, (and without this the best medicine will go down, or rather will not go up,) they push to a great extent by the aid of capital, and they gain in reputation and keep what they have. Among this class Dr. G. Benj. Smith's "Sugar-coated Indian Vegetable Pills" (of which General Taylor has spoken highly) stand pre-eminent. Without making any excitement, they were rapidly put out over the United States and Canada four or five years ago, and they have since been gradually pushed and thoroughly established, by a system of agencies, into every little village. If it be any evidence of a good medicine that no one calls it a humbug, then these Pills stand high, for such a charge has yet to be made against them. At all events they have a large sale and are managed with a degree of respectability not common to this branch of trade.

Dr. Sherman's medicines, although they have gone down, enabled him to build up-town, and he finally got up a Panorama for exhibition. Townshend is supposed to be realizing a fortune; and Dr. Moffat's medicines are still a source of some revenue, as also Dr. Brandreth's, while each are variously engaged in other speculations, which they are enabled to carry on upon the fruits of the Patent Medicine business.

We copy the following from a late number of a medical paper:—

"When a Physician so far forgets the feelings of humanity that should always predominate in his practice, and uses his profession as a cloak to amass a fortune, he generally accomplishes his object, like Dr. MORRISON of London, the inventor of the 'Hygean Pills.' These Pills were put up in packages of three boxes each, numbered one, two, and three, and to be taken in regular order; holding out the impression that they contained three different kinds of medicine. These Pills became at one time quite popular in the United States, till the general agent's sale in New England was one hundred dollars a day, when he, becoming an extensive counterfeiter of them, had to leave the place. It was afterwards proved that these Pills were made in New York, and that number one, two, and three, were all the same article. The medical faculty came out in London and stated that Mr. Morrison was destroying much life by the recommendation of such quantities of medicine. He prosecuted the faculty for libel, and in every instance was beaten. In fifteen years he amassed a princely fortune, built himself a palace with the hope of enjoying his wealth, but an overruling Providence has called him to that bourne from whence no traveller returns, there to give an account of his doings, and to meet those from whom he had extorted much of his wealth.

DR. BRANDRETH came out here from London, about five years after Morrison's Pills became popular, and established the sale of his Pills, adopting Morrison's plan of recommending every one to take his Pills in great quantities, and he has accumulated a fortune. He gave the agency in Pennsylvania to Mr. Wright, a brother Englishman, for a number of years; when his sales became very extensive he got up a counterfeit, which caused Mr. Brandreth to take away the Agency from him, when he changed the name of the counterfeit Pills and called them "Indian Vegetable Pills," and got a number of Brandreth's Travelling Agents to put them out in the country. Another Englishman got up a Pill called "Old Parr's," stating that he lived one hundred and fifty years on his Pills. The story was too absurd to be believed, and they found little or no sale. There are quite a number of other Pills pretending to come out from Europe, but are made in the United States, and have proved a failure.

Several Physicians have adopted the course of Morrison of London by manufacturing many articles to be taken for the same complaint. A Physician located himself in Broadway, New York, issues his handbills monthly, stating the day he would be in Boston, Lowell, Providence, Fall River, New Bedford, Norwich Town, New York, Troy, Albany, and Hudson, for consultation, gratis.

The secret of this Doctor's success, has grown solely out of his vituperations against the medical faculty; branding them with ignorance, as possessing no medical skill, intended to be understood by the afflicted; that they all go in for making the most money out of the sick, except himself, who is the only "Good Samaritan," and filled with philanthropy for the distressed. Whilst the truth is, the most of his money is wrung out of the poor, who too often have to obtain through charity the means to purchase his extravagant medicines; whilst he tells them in all cases, they have the liver complaint—that being curable—when he knows they are in a consumption and no relief can be had for them.

It is to be regretted that such a large portion of our classical scholars run into the medical profession, as our large cities are crowded, and there are ten to do the practice that was done formerly by one; which has induced many to adopt the method of travelling from place to place, and give advice gratis, but charge extravagantly for their medicines, and relying upon excitement for their practice, as the opportunities to pronounce them sick, when little or nothing ails them, is too great to be resisted; and it would be well for persons to listen to these travelling Doctors with ears both open, but with their hands on their pockets, for fear their money may be magnetized from them, as these travelling Doctors are constantly increasing, and receive encouragement from persons attending their lectures, and other various modes of making their appearance known."

A distinguished writer on health once said, "Much as I place my trust in diet and regimen, I bow with submission to the noble art of healing, and cling to it for succor." It is good for us to be a little sick occasionally, for

"Who never ails, health never knows."

And it verily appears that health can only be properly estimated when sickness comes upon us. It is well that pain admonishes us early, when we have violated nature's simplest laws; and in conclusion, let me advise the reader to study the best mode of living to avoid quackery in all shapes; then

"Learn to suffer what you cannot shun."

Slice XXX.—BALLS AND BELLES OF TAMMANY HALL.

URIOUS reader, now that we have taken a pretty wide range through the City, slicing off here and there a chip or a fragment as we went along, and endeavoring so to show you something of what Civilization can produce when it tries its best—and its worse—it is time that we should take a little innocent recreation. Hard work and bitter scenes have we passed through in these our rambles, yet ever contemplating some good to poor human nature. Now let us repose awhile and look in upon lighter and more joyous scenes. Because the world is so afflicted with foul diseases, with dire sufferings, and hopeless crimes, we are not to suppose that there is nothing gay and bright and happy, left for us to contemplate. Therefore, dear reader, whoever thou art—grave and earnest, with mouth and eyes agape for statistics of trade or quotations of stock; light and trifling as the hopes and aims of youth, or bright and balmy as the blue eye and white bosom of young maidenhood—whoever thou art that hast gone with us through these free pencillings of scenes and character in this great, dirty, blustering, glorious, ill-lighted, aristocratic, squalid, rich, wicked, and magnificent metropolis—did you ever go to a ball at Tammany Hall? If not, then are you, by inexpressibly long odds, the greenest greenhorn in the Universe—greener than green ointment or the man that bid off a gold lever watch yesterday in Broadway for ten dollars. But remain in this wretched state no longer. The season is now fast coming on for these grand flare-ups, and we shall have one at least every night. You can find them at all prices, from the aristocratic affair of the Democratic General Committee, at which Vice President Dallas and champagne are the order of the night, to the dollar jubilee of "No. —," with its bouncing b'hoys, plump and bright-eyed girls, and the modest bill of fare in the restaurant. In a few weeks those fearful blood-red globes upon the balcony will stream their crimson lustre into the very eyes of the night,—through the half uncurtained windows will be caught dreary glimpses of graceful or Herculean forms, and across the brown and breezy Park will float the music—mellowed by the distance and a bath in the keen and sparkling night air—of three fiddles, two horns, a trombone, and a wry-necked piccolo. Let us therefore anticipate a little the gay time that is to come, and describe in advance some of the merry scenes which will jump into existence behind those gleaming, fiery balls of light.

Dancing is a universal human instinct; and Gall and Spurzheim—who by the way stole their theory from Swedenborg—committed a grave error in not assigning it a distinctive bump in the cranium. In women the organ is almost always "active," while with men it exists in a dormant state and depends very much on "circumstances" for its exercise and development. It is remarkable, too, that all classes of women dance with nearly equal grace and ease, while with men there are few of any grade who ever rise to mediocrity in the bewitching art. Men have a thousand other ways—and most of them worse ones—of getting rid of their superabundant excitability and animal spirits, while with women dancing is every thing. A woman dances into love and dances out of it. She fixes her destiny for life in the pauses of a quadrille; and the fascinations of the last polka have frequently lost her the world, her own honor, and a respectable epitaph. To a vast number of women, in all ranks of society, life is a commonplace, unmeaning interval between dances.—The lady of fashion pads and rouges, spends a fortune in costume and cosmetics, and neglects her own duties and her children's education, that she may shine with irresistible splendor in the dance. In other ranks the pretty book-folder and the pale seamstress, the buxom housemaid and the ambitious laundress, slave cheerfully all the week in the dreariest and most monotonous occupations, that they may obtain the means of making a handsome appearance at the Saturday night dance. The malefactor and his degraded companion, hunted by the Police and a price set upon their heads—seek the glaring cellar in the Five Points, and in the excitement of the dance forget for a moment their infamy and

PARK—CITY HALL.

their danger. So we see that, in whatever circumstances we may be placed, an all-prevailing impulse to put one's self into violent bodily exercise to any sort of an imitation of music, is sure to manifest itself.

But however general may be the impulse to dance, it is at Tammany Hall that the heartiest, most genial, and altogether the thoroughest enjoyment of this inspiring pastime is to be witnessed. The balls at this establishment may be taken as the perfected type of a class of amusements entirely characteristic of New York, and to be met with nowhere else. It is usual for poor people to entertain a certain degree of envy for the amusements and dissipations of the rich; but we are sure that no ray of that bad feeling ever found its way into the spacious dancing saloon of Tammany Hall. There, all who enter come to give and receive pleasure; and the idea that there *can* be a more superb room for dancing, or a more sumptuous entertainment, never enters anybody's head.

What first strikes you upon entering the ball-room is the variety of costume. No one style predominates—every one seeming to have consulted her own individual, independent taste, with but faint reference to those infallible guides to tip-top gentility, the magazine fashion-plates. Crimson velvet boddices, and green barege skirts; long sleeves, short sleeves, and no sleeves; the balloon, the sack, the long dress, the short dress, the high and the low; all are intermingled, like a fancy ball fallen into a doze and confounding its costumes in a sort of wild dream-mixture. The only uniformity you see is in every woman having a pair of blooming cheeks and sparkling eyes, all glowing and beaming with happiness. The conversation and manners are free, and yet perfectly respectful and polite. The male portion of the assembly are apt to be somewhat of the roughest; and the bar-room is filled with drinkers, and smokers, and tobacco-chewers, equally ready for an argument, a smasher, or a fight. But up-stairs every thing is entirely changed; and, as a general thing, affairs are conducted in the most exemplary manner.

Some of our readers may perhaps suppose that the dances at Tammany Hall are a little antiquated, and lack the fascinating freshness which imparts so agreeable an atmosphere to the *soirées dansantes* of "Above Bleecker." But this is not the case. Since the invention of the Magnetic Telegraph, and the Revolution of February, Tammany Hall is as near Paris as Union Square; and no new dance can make half-a-dozen gyrations in our aristocratic drawing-rooms before it is caught up and repeated in a style somewhat exaggerated, but far more exhilarating, on the bounding boards of Tammany Hall. It is true that the good old-fashioned cotillion and even the jig and break-down, are not entirely abandoned; but there is no lack of ambitious couples, gorgeous in brilliant vest and flying ribbon-streamers of many colors, standing ready on shore eager to take advantage of the first opening between the undulations of the crowded floor, and plunge off like a pair of adventurous bathers into all sorts of gyroflexions, polka-ish, or otherwise. Gradually, couple by couple, the many tire and glide off reeling to their seats, or to seek refreshment in the restaurant; but an ambitious couple—the "Mose" and "Lize" of the evening—still keep it up with unflagging fervor, seeming to increase their momentum at every whirl. The company now gather round and begin to be excited. The plot thickens, and the game is made up. It is muscle and sinew against horsehair and catgut. For a few minutes the race is as even as that of two steamers on the Hudson; but soon the elbow-power of the principal fiddler begins to relax—his tones come forth more and more feeble, and his tortured instrument gives a piercing and unearthly scream every time it comes to "the turn of the tune." Meanwhile upon the floor the fun grows "fast and furious"—the spectators applaud, the dancers redouble their exertions, their faces glowing like glass-blowers, or like lovers caught kissing. At last the despairing fiddler claps his left thumb and forefinger to the nut of his E string—snap! pop! it is gone—the dance is finished and he saves his reputation.

But if the dancing part of the business is characteristic, the manner of supping and serving refreshments is no less so. Instead of the clumsy, inconvenient and altogether vexatious method usually employed, of crowding every thing on a long table and driving the company down all at once to take a standee and a cold cut here and there of something they don't like, while every one sees his favorite dish disappearing down somebody else's throat—at Tammany Hall you select the time most agreeable to yourself or your partner, slip quietly with your lady down stairs, take a comfortable seat at a little table in the Restaurant, and order whatever you like, from a shilling stew and brandy without, to a canvass-back and champagne. Here there are none to crowd you from your places, squeeze you to calf's jelly, nor overhear every thing you choose to say; and for a nice, quiet, comfortable bit of love-making—a thing which of all others we admire—there cannot be a more fitting place nor a more favorable opportunity than while taking your supper at a Tammany Hall ball.

By midnight everybody has had supper and is ready to renew the serious business of the night, and dancing is resumed with fourfold spirit, and kept up without intermission until four o'clock, when the party breaks up and the grand rush for cloaks, hoods, and carriages, takes place. The delicate scramble attending this dainty operation is by no means the least interesting and exciting part of the performances. Many a tender squeeze of the hand, and even innocent kiss, is exchanged between the owners of fluttering hearts, in the dim passages leading to the dressing-rooms; and many the pouting denial and unexpected rebuff also encountered here. At length the last pair of "fantastic toes," with their pretty owner and her beau, have disappeared within the last cab, which whirls grumbling and creaking with the cold up Chatham-street—the blood-red meteors on the balcony suddenly go out in darkness—the Boots seizes the occasion to lock the front door—the bar-keeper crawls yawning up stairs to bed—and Tammany Hall, lately so gay and brilliant, is as dark and solitary as if it had just got news of a Whig victory.

Slice XXXI.—THE AMERICAN ART-UNION.

Come, dear reader, we have "supped full of horrors"—let us leave the sad and depressing task of dissecting the foulness and corruption engendered in a large city. Let us now recreate ourselves with a lighter labor, and pause for a moment to admire the ideal beautiful, and permit the divine and soothing influences of Art to steal into our souls. Step with us into this long and smoothly-lighted gallery, opening conveniently from Broadway, and crowded with well-dressed ladies and gentlemen. This is the Free Gallery of the American Art-Union—an institution devoted exclusively to the cultivation of the fine arts, and which has risen to wealth and wide reputation in a very few years, from very small beginnings. At first its income was scarcely over twenty-five hundred dollars a year—now it amounts to near a hundred thousand. A very handsome business, truly!

The honor of first having applied the immense moral lever of combined effort and means to the advancement of the fine arts, belongs to Germany. It was there that, in 1823, Art-Unions were invented, and the first one established at Munich, which avowed for its object the promotion of modern art and the encouragement of rising merit, by the purchase of pictures. The Berlin Association, which owed its existence principally to the efforts of the celebrated William Humboldt, who was its first President, and with whom were associated the sculptors Rauch and Tieck, the architect Schinkel, the painters Wach and Schadow, and other distinguished men. The success of these two associations stimulated the ambition of other parts of Germany, until in 1839 the number of Art-Unions was twenty-nine, with an annual aggregate income of over one hundred thousand dollars. In 1837 the London Art-Union was established, and its annual income, at first small, in 1846 exceeded seventeen thousand pounds sterling. Edinburg, Dublin, Manchester, Birmingham, and other British cities, each has also its flourishing Art-Union. In our own country, we have, in addition to the American Art-Union, similar institutions in Philadelphia, Boston, and Cincinnati; and as these pages are being written, a prospectus has been issued for an International Art-Union, to purchase and distribute foreign pictures and works of art, to establish a free gallery of the works of modern Europe, and to send every year an American artist to study in Europe.

The plan of all these associations is essentially the same. "Each subscriber pays some small amount annually. This forms a fund, which, after defraying necessary expenses, is appropriated to the production of engravings, and the purchase of works of art. The engravings are given to all the subscribers, and the other works of art are distributed among them by lot. In the London association, money prizes are allotted instead of paintings, the holders being required to expend the money in the purchase of works from certain specified exhibitions. This plan has been adopted by the Philadelphia association. In nearly all the others, however, the works distributed are selected by the managing committees; and an attempt is now being made by the Board of Trade, which has the supervision of the London Society, to have the same method adopted there.

Museum. BROADWAY. Astor-House.

"The American Art-Union is the only one in this country, which, from the extent of its operations, and the amount of its resources, can be called a national institution. Its history is a striking proof of the peculiar adaptation of its plan to the character and circumstances of our people. The rapidity with which it has grown in public favor, is altogether unprecedented. At the first anniversary meeting in December, 1839, the number of subscribers for that year was stated to be eight hundred and fourteen, and the amount received from them, four thousand one hundred and forty-five dollars. In 1841, the number of subscribers was nine hundred and thirty-seven, and but seven works of art were distributed. Six years afterwards, in 1847, the subscribers had increased to nine thousand six hundred and sixty-six; the receipts to forty-eight thousand seven hundred and thirty-three dollars and ninety-one cents, while nearly three hundred paintings were distributed, besides hundreds of medals in silver and bronze. Its prosperity during the present year is still more remarkable. The Bulletin of October 10th states, that for the few weeks previous to that date, the subscriptions were four times as many as they were the last year during the corresponding period. A list of from twelve to fifteen thousand is confidently anticipated; but the committee have determined, that whenever so much money is received as can be judiciously invested in paintings, the books will be peremptorily closed, although subscriptions received afterwards will be entered in their order at the head of the list for 1849."*

The distribution of the American Art-Union for this year is uncommonly rich, and very naturally attracts great attention. The Annual Engraving is to be from Huntington's picture of "Queen Mary Signing the Death-Warrant of Lady Jane Grey;" and besides this, every subscriber will receive a copy of the new edition of Irving's "Rip Van Winkle," illustrated by the exquisite pencil of Darley. The paintings and works of art already purchased for distribution during the present year, amount to nearly three hundred. Among them is the series of four allegorical pictures by Cole, the "Voyage of Life," painted for Mr. Ward, and for which the artist received six thousand dollars. There are also two fine landscapes by Durand; the Mission of the Jews to Ferdinand and Isabella, by Leutze; the Strolling Musician, by Edmonds; the Queen Mary of Huntington, (from which the Annual Engraving is being made,) the River of the Water of Life, by Church, the pupil of Cole; a superb moonlight winter scene by Doughty; with pictures of rare merit by Grey, Rossiter, Gignoux, Chapman, Kensett, Cropsey, Hinckley, May, Wenzler, Audubon, Glass, Duggan, Oddie, Peele, White, and others. In addition to the pictures, a series of valuable medals is distributed annually among the subscribers. The medal for the present year is a bust of the celebrated portrait-painter Gilbert Stewart. Two hundred and fifty copies of this will be distributed, as well as two hundred of the Allston medals of 1847, which have been so much admired.

We have thus devoted an entire number of our series of City Sketches to a single institution—fearless of being accused of partiality by any who rightly appreciate the influences of the fine arts upon the morals and refinement of mankind.

* Knickerbocker for November.

Slice XXXII.—THE ARTISTS' ART-UNION.

We know not whether this be the proper title under which to notice a laudable effort now being made, by several distinguished artists, to form an Association for the purpose of promoting the production of Historical Paintings, such as those of the Italian and Flemish schools. The American Art-Union does not require works that are too large for dwelling-houses: but as works of larger size are better for exhibitions, and for public buildings, the artists think it expedient to attempt a new organization for the purpose of giving this direction to the efforts of American genius.

They are to establish a gallery, to be open during the whole year, as a place in which artists can show their works to the public, and dispose of them by direct sale.

During part of the time their exhibition is to be a paying one; the proceeds to be shared by those who furnish the works, in proportion to the value of those works, for exhibition purposes.

There is to be a provision for artists of merit, who, from infirmity or other misfortune, are unable to live with the comfort they deserve. But this provision is not to be wholly a matter of charity. It is intended to deduct from the receipts a certain percentage, which is to be added to the capital of the institution, and to remain in it forever as capital, unless any one who had contributed should be in the condition above mentioned; in which case he would be allowed to draw out his part of it, in such sums as his wants might require. And that part which pertains to those who are not thus in want is to pay interest, (or profit,) to them or their heirs, so long as the Institution shall exist, and to be drawn out only on the closing up of its concerns.

In addition to this, there is to be a Benevolent Fund, composed of donations, and of the proceeds of the exhibition of such works as may be loaned to the Institution for the benefit of that fund; those works to be valued like the rest.

As to the authority by which these values shall be determined, we do not learn that it is yet agreed on: but some, fearing that displeasure and secession would result from any mode of valuation among the associates themselves, think it best to choose from among connoisseurs a certain number to whom this appraisal may be committed; and to prevent the dissatisfaction that might be felt, from causing any to withdraw, they think that no person should serve a second time in that capacity.

If this plan should be successfully carried out in this city, it is intended to extend it to other parts, and invite the co-operation of other artists; and to have the works circulate, so that each shall be seen in all the principal cities. Besides giving their works the best opportunity of becoming known and purchased, it is thought that this system of exhibition will cause the production of works of that class which the Venetian and Florentine artists excelled in; works of such dimensions as are too great for private houses, and suited only to exhibitions.

As to the use of that capital which may result from the percentage of the general receipts, it is intended to loan it to artists who have works in the exhibition, but in sums that are clearly less than the market value of those works, so that the institution may not be exposed to loss. And it is intended that the institution shall act as the custodier of works, in case artists wish to borrow money upon them from private persons. Thus an ambitious artist, having expended all he had or could borrow upon one great work, instead of being embarrassed for the next five years, would be enabled to commence another at once, and so to continue his labors.

More might be said, had we room, in favor of the views thus briefly sketched; but we can only give a glance at the means of so filling a gallery as to bring together enough *paying* lovers of art to furnish the money needful for the operations in the somewhat magnificent prospective. Looking at the works shown in the present exhibitions, we feel some confidence that the *natural capacity* for becoming great artists does exist, in many cases; but the practice in small, cheap, popular pictures, will not soon make a Titian, a Correggio, a Raffaelle, a Paul Veronese, or any other great artist: to develope such powers we must put them on great undertakings, and *keep* them constantly employed on them. If this be done, we feel assured that the refined portion of the community will find such a gallery worth visiting, and worth paying for.

In connection with this subject we deem it proper to notice an artist who has recently returned from Italy, bringing with him many copies, by himself, from the best works of the Venetians, Correggio, and others. We allude to Mr. J. K. Fisher. He has copies of the following pictures:—by Titian, the Assumption of the Virgin, the Presentation of the Virgin at the Temple, the Peter Martyr, Cain and Abel, David and Goliath, the two Venuses of the Florentine Gallery, the Danae of the Museum in Naples, the Three Graces, Sacred and Profane Love, and several others; by Correggio, the St. Jerome, the Danae, the Madonna del Coniglio, the Marriage of St. Catharine, and some sketches; by Paul Veronese, four of his principal pictures in Venice, and three in Rome and Florence; by Tintoretto, tho Crucifixion, and the Miracle of the Slave, esteemed as his two best works; by Raffaelle, the Incendio del Borgo; by Daniel di Volterra, the Descent from the Cross; and numerous small copies and sketches from the best colorists. He is one of those who are in favor of this movement; and, as his collection is composed of copies, of liberal size, from works of the highest excellence, we think he will be a welcome contributor to a gallery which regards the wants of true taste, so far as to admit something that will give us an idea of the great masters, whose original works are nowhere to be found in this country.

In point of execution and coloring, these copies are regarded as excellent, by the professional and other connoisseurs who have seen them. We do not hesitate to say that none better have been brought to this country. The original works of this artist show that he has imbibed the principles of the Venetian colorists: indeed, some of them are praised as copies from the great masters, by those who do not know whom they were designed by.

Mr. Fisher is glad to receive the visits of artists, and the friends of art, whenever he is not engaged with sitters. We advise all such to avail themselves of the opportunity to see a collection which, if not of so much account in the market as "undoubted originals" would be, is far more acceptable to true taste than the works we have seen here, called by the names of Titian, Raffaelle, Rubens, &c. His rooms are at No. 179 Broadway.

Slice XXXIII.—THE BOWERY.

If our Muse would condescend to array herself in a bright red shawl, *two* hair-cloth skirts, and a bonnet, whose periphery, sectionally and horizontally, should be on a parallel with the acute point of the angle of her nose, we might hope that she would inspire us with some worthy description of the Bowery; but as there is no hope of a poor scribbler having any such honor, while the b'hoys are so plenty, and wear such fiery red shirts, and drive such fast nags, and chew such gigantic quids of tobacco, we must content ourselves—and we hope our readers—with plain prose. Not to mention, then, the Bowery Theatre, the grand National Circus on the other side, Vauxhall and its dependencies, we may simply characterize the Bowery as the place where slang comes from. "Well, it ain't any thing else!" "Why don't you come along!"

If one would get a correct idea of what the Bowery boys and gals can do, when they put their best foot forward, let him attend the Bowery Theatre on New Year's or Christmas eve. The whole immense area of the house looks like a hot-bed of exotic and high-colored plants and flowers, packed so closely together that it is difficult to conceive how a breath of air ever finds its way between them. But to judge from the noisy lung-exercise of the evening, in which all classes participate, and seem emulous to see who can contribute most to swell the merry and riotous chorus, as to the performances on the stage, they are neither here nor there. Compared with the performances in the audience, the ranting and bellowing and spasmodic galvanism of the actors on the stage, are quite tame and commonplace. "Hello, Bill Swipes! You up in the second tier! Who de —— guv yer de extra shillin'?" "Come out of that, you Jo Brewer! Why don't yer come along!" "I say, Jim! ain't this high? Have yer salooned yer gal yet?" "Get off my toes! Keep yer ——— sharp elbows out o' my ribs! Take that be J——! Watch! murder! Take him off! Hyst der rag! Go it! Sh-sh-sh-h-h!" and so up goes the curtain, the orchestra blows and kicks, and the actors go on in perfect dumb-show—not a syllable nor a squeak being heard by the uproarious, joyous audience.

The Bowery has its "fashionable side," too, as well as Broadway; and here, in fine weather, you may see a procession of absolutely the handsomest women in America. Red cheeks and lips, eyes sparkling, and round ripe forms palpitating with health, and that exuberant fullness of life which makes the chief fascination in woman, and which fashionable dissipation so soon destroys—these are the characteristics of Bowery beauty. It may be true that these plump and hearty divinities betray some little *bizarrerie* in the selection of colors and the cut of their dresses, yet they believe that it is exactly the thing; and whenever they take the trouble to think of the poor pale-faced creatures of Broadway, they actually and heartily pity them.

The Bowery is celebrated for its drinking and gambling-houses, its poultry-raffling shops, and its "crack" ice-cream saloons. It is the grand parade-ground of the "b'hoys" and "g'hals," the arena where "high-life below stairs" makes its grandest demonstrations; and to a philosopher a walk through the Bowery would furnish abundant food for thought and contemplation.

The business operations of the Bowery, although they are generally somewhat lost sight of under the "highfaluting" reputation of that celebrated thoroughfare, are nevertheless of no insignificant nor unvaried character. In fact, every careful housewife in New York can inform you that you can purchase any conceivable article you may stand in need of, from an apple-sauce-kettle to a baby's cap, at least twenty-five per cent. cheaper and better in the Bowery than anywhere else in the city. And as for Hats and Boots, and especially Ready-made Clothing, a man must be a perfect green-horn who would think of going anywhere else to spend his money.

Why, it is only the other day—just before getting ready to make our New Year's calls—that, finding our best black coat rather seedy at the elbows, our don't-know-what-to-call-'ems grievously afflicted with "knee-holes," and our waistcoat minus several of its most important buttons, we dropped in upon our friend Stiles—Captain Stiles—at the corner of Walker-street and the Bowery. Such forests of pantaloons! Such oceans of waistcoats! Such plantations of faultless coats! The only difficulty we encountered was in making a choice from such a superabundance of elegance. And as for money—why that was positively no object at all. Having taken with us about the usual price of a suit of "extra black superfine," we discovered, after laying aside, and paying for every thing we wanted for a complete rig, that we had money enough left to fit out our eldest son—a good strapping chunk of a boy of eighteen—with a complete suit from top to toe, and to supply our youngest daughter with spending-money for the best part of a quarter. It is true that this is perhaps the *most* extensive and complete establishment of the kind either in the Bowery or the city; and to which all classes of population rush for their supplies of clothing. Yet there are hundreds of other large concerns in the Bowery well worth especial consideration—if we only had plenty of time and money. Captain Stiles himself, the principal of the establishment we have been mentioning, is a man whose personal history is romantic and interesting enough to form a chapter by itself; but as we haven't yet arrived at the biographical phase of our literary existence, all this must be passed over, until, as Dogberry says, "there be no need of such vanities."

In the upper part of the Bowery we are arrested by a crowd standing in front of a large show-window of a looking-glass and frame warehouse, between Spring and Prince streets. This is the famous Looking-glass and Picture-frame Manufactory of Mr. Johnson, 204 Bowery—where every variety of these articles is not only sold but manufactured, in the most exquisite and perfect manner. His location in the Bowery subjecting him to far less expense in the way of rent, &c., than the pretentious and *soi-disant* fashionable dealers, he is not only able to furnish, but does furnish every article in his line from 10 to 20 per cent. cheaper than other and more showy establishments. It is a fact perfectly self-evident, that the proprietors of these gorgeous and expensive establishments expect to receive the interest on the capital thus locked up in useless embellishments, out of the pockets of their customers. To judge from the great success of

Mr. Johnson's establishment during the few past years, these facts appear to be pretty well understood.

If we step inside of this establishment, we shall find the most complete stock of looking-glasses, of every sort and size, from 12½ cts. to $200, many of them of the newest and most brilliant styles and patterns. The picture-frame department, too, is most extensive and complete, and the whole establishment is well worth visiting by those who wish to *buy*. But to return to the window.

The most striking features of the place, however, are the *features* of gentlemen and ladies, so naturally and truthfully painted as to startle the spectator into the belief that he sees before him real men and women encased in frames. These portraits are the production of Messrs. Miller and Hillyer, who have acquired a reputation, within a few years past, for *accuracy* and *expression* in their portraits, second to none in the country. Their painting-rooms are at 16 Rivington-street, a few doors east of the Bowery.

These gentlemen attribute their great success in portrait-painting to their peculiar method, which is a division of labor and study in each portrait—the department of one artist being *drawing*, that of the other *color;* while both combine, in mutual criticism and suggestion, to produce that animated identity of expression, without which, however well executed, a portrait may be a mere map of the face.

The advantage which they derive from this novel co-operation in art is, that while it relieves each artist from the fatigue and blunted perceptions which invariably attend a too long and tedious study of the same subject, it also assists them in giving to each sitting an easy, conversational, at-home sort of character, which develops the more familiar expression of countenance so desirable to the intimate friends and relatives of the original, and, by a natural consequence, requiring fewer and less tedious sittings, and exempting from the necessity of after-corrections and alterations.

Availing themselves of the assistance of a skilful artist in painting their draperies, backgrounds, &c., Messrs. Miller and Hillyer confine their attention entirely to the likeness, and the result has met their most sanguine anticipations.

These artists aim simply at *characteristic portraiture;* and those who desire, under the name of portraits, merely pretty pictures or artistic affectations, will of course go where they can obtain them. They are well convinced by past experience that daily study and practice will best enable them to sustain their present reputation for Faithful Likeness, and that a moderate rate of charges is most likely to supply them with that full practice which they require. Thus they have resisted every temptation to increase their charges, offered by the flattering extent of their reputation, and continue to believe that they are better and more satisfactorily remunerated, while at the same time much more agreeably employed, than they could be with fewer pictures and higher prices.

Having long since observed the fact, that a satisfactory portrait is productive property to the artist for years after it has passed out of his possession, while an unsatisfactory one under the same circumstances is a constant source of injury, they have established a rule on the subject which they intend to abide by,—that they will allow no portrait to leave their possession until its likeness is fairly tested, and will receive payment for no picture unless accompanied by unequivocal expression of satisfaction. This is taking strong ground; but they refer, with a justifiable pride, to the possessors of more than five hundred of their portraits in this city and its vicinity (many of them copies made after death from daguerreotypes) for their cheerful corroboration of the fact.

There! For a good, strong, sensible piece of artistic criticism, we think that will match Kit North or John Neal; and Messrs. Miller and Hillyer may bless their lucky stars for the chance that brought The Slicer among the crowd before their lifelike pictures. Henceforth they are as famous as they deserve to be. Could more be said?

Good-by, Bowery! We might linger for many and many a page amid thy piquant and exciting scenes; but even as we lay down our pen to light our last "Leone d'Oro," and puff away care, a grim-visaged imp appeareth at our den-window, holding out both hands for copy, and exclaiming, "Why don't you come along—s-a-y!"

Slice XXXIV.—MANUFACTURES OF NEW YORK.

We might as well undertake to record the names of all the applicants for office under General Taylor on our thumb-nail, as to give any adequate idea of the extent, variety and importance of the Manufactures of New York in a single "Slice." Yet we could not justify ourselves for entirely neglecting all mention of so vast an element of the wealth and greatness of the metropolis—an element which events in every direction conspire to increase to gigantic proportions. Already the current of those changes and improvements has strongly set in, which will constitute New York still more decidedly than now the centre and capital of the Union—the brain, the heart, the pulse, whence flow and to which return all the vital forces that go to make up the life, health and vigor of a mighty empire. The converging lines of railroad and steamboat transportation, of domestic and foreign import and export, of home and outward travel, already make New York the grand depot and entrepot of the Union; while its vast local and foreign commerce, its immense pecuniary resources and incalculable enterprise, make its voice omnipotent and final in all questions of finance and political economy.

In intellectual and moral questions, the fiat of New York is no less powerful and no less regarded by the provincial portions of the republic. Her Press alone employs a greater amount of actual practical talent than can be collected elsewhere in all the Union; while her Bar, her Bench, her Pulpit, and the ranks of Literature and the other professions embrace a variety and extent of intellectual power unequalled perhaps throughout the old world. Having already gained so much momentum, the ranks of all these classes are constantly being strengthened by accessions of the most brilliant individuals in other cities or remote districts, who, inspired by the only real ambition, rush to the great intellectual focus of the age, to compete where victory is honor and to shine where all is bright.

But a not less important and integral portion of the true greatness and solidity of New York is its colossal and rapidly-increasing manufacturing interest. Other places, possessing no other available elements, are wont to brag largely and make immense ados over their manufacturing operations; while, if the facts and figures were stated, they would, even in their favorite and only point, be so completely overshadowed by the manufactures of our huge Babel, that the contrast would become simply ridiculous. Our Cotton, Woollen, Iron and Flour Manufactories, our Machine and Engine and Boiler Foundries, our Steamboat and Ship building, would readily furnish a list of names and a sum total of capital that would make Major Downing open his eyes as wide as platters just to look over. But we have no intention of performing so unnecessary a work as this, nor even if we had, would it be possible under a year's hard work to do any thing like justice in such a list to all the innumerable interests that would crowd in to swell it to the dimensions of a directory.

But sometimes greater men than ourselves have got over a difficulty, arising from the immenseness of their subject, by concentrating all their powers of description upon one or two specimens—somewhat on the principle—although we hope in our case with a more satisfactory result—of the real estate speculator who carried a brick as a sample of the house he had for sale. Whether he carried the brick in his hat or not, we have not been able to learn.

And as we know of no better guide to recommend us to the right selection of this specimen than to describe the establishments which in the course of our investigations have most strikingly excited our admiration, we shall endeavor to convey to the reader some faint idea of that immense and almost perfect establishment, the *Croton Flour Mills,* of Hecker & Brother, in Cherry-street, near Pike. There is apparent throughout the whole of this establishment the presence, as it were, of a conscious Intelligence and Will, which guides the innumerable, delicate and complicated operations of the whole, with the certainty, promptness and celerity of the human body. Two words will embody this gigantic and beautiful spirit—Energy and Compactness. We confess that we never felt so forcibly the true character and destiny of the present age—to embody and make practical the poetry, philosophy and power of human nature for the good of man—as when standing amid the countless wheels and movements of this little world of scientific and a-meal-iorative (we *must* have our joke, which Messrs. Hecker may *bolt* or not, as they please) industry of inert matter. Not an inch of room, not an ounce of power, nor a moment of time, is wasted throughout the whole building. As we enter, a load of Wheat is discharging into the iron grating over the sidewalk, while the ever-busy elevators are carrying it steadily and quietly into the upper portions of the building, and depositing it without the aid of hands, in its appropriate receptacles. We enter the compact and well-arranged counting-house, where mountains of books and papers are disposed of so orderly as not to give the slightest idea of accumulation. It is warmed by a congeries of iron pipes conveying the *exhausted steam,* which is thus made to perform one more kindly office for man before spreading its white wings, and hiding behind the blue curtains of the air, like Ariel at last escaping from enthralment.

Instead of mounting, tired and panting like a defeated racehorse, unending flights of stairs, we step upon a platform and touch a little iron handle, when, lo! into the upper regions we move as smoothly and silently as if mounted on the back of some stout bird, who sets us down quietly, at a touch, wherever we will. We are quite sure that if all the benevolent hotel-keepers would only visit the Croton Mills, and see these two operations of heating rooms and getting up and down stairs, they would at once adopt them throughout their establishments. What weary legs and backs of boarders and servants, and what shivering over half-built fires, what carrying of coal and ashes, what scolding of impatient ladies, what sorrow and affliction of all sorts arising from a deficiency of caloric, would not be thus avoided!

The very genius of the Croton Mills is Improvement; and in doing its work, a spirit of boldness, liberality and independence is manifested, which of itself makes the establishment worthy of especial notice. If a new and important discovery is made in machinery, or in any thing coming within the sphere of their business, the Messrs. Hecker do not, as is almost always the case, reject it because it is new—but they give it a thorough, searching examination. If it receives the approbation of their own judgment, (which is seldom at fault,) it is tested on a small scale; and if found to answer, and to be *really* an improvement, it is at once adopted throughout the establishment, no matter what the expense. Thus, the substitution of bands for cog-wheels as immediate motor powers where vast and complicated motions were required, was boldly adopted by Messrs. Hecker & Brother, and with the most brilliant result. Not a cog-wheel hums and buzzes and clanks and tortures the ear in the whole establishment; and thus a constant and excruciating nuisance is avoided, while a large saving of room and power is effected. A little while ago Gutta Percha round bands were proposed instead of leather; and, although generally rejected at first by other establishments, yet the Croton Mills found that they were a great improvement, bound eventually to supersede leather entirely, and consequently at once commenced adopting them. By a happy thought of Mr. Hecker himself, in adjusting the stretch of the band and the resistance of the pulley at exactly the right point, the band is prevented entirely from slipping, heating, and melting; and thus the only shadow of an objection ever brought against Gutta Percha, is obviated.

The same spirit—ever on the alert for discoveries and improvements—is manifest especially in the engine department of these mills. The steam is generated in an improved model called the *Montgomery Boiler*, which consists of a series of tubes, through which a constant circulation is maintained; and presenting a much larger amount of surface to the action of the fire than in the ordinary construction, of course greatly reduces the expense of fuel. We are not scientific enough to describe this boiler, only to say that it is like the human brain, with its economy of convolutions, carried out in sheet-iron tubes; the fire corresponding to the nervous *aura*, which like an unseen flame plays among and warms them with vital heat. A still bolder and more brilliant triumph is about to be achieved by Messrs. Hecker. Notwithstanding that the Oscillating Engine has been extensively condemned, yet Messrs. Hecker became satisfied that the principle was a good one; and by improvements of Mr. Henry Waterman, machinist, which we wish we were learned enough to describe, he has obviated the only objections to the Oscillator, and is now engaged in manufacturing a gigantic engine on this principle, soon to take the place of the one in use, effecting an important saving.

In short, we cannot better describe the whole spirit and materiel of this establishment than by saying that it is an epitome of the Anglo-Saxon character and race—vigorous, inquiring, daring, energetic, untiring, improving—the race to whom Nature has confided the task of bearing the world onward in its grand progress through the present century.

We have not spoken of the details of the Croton Mills—nor do we well know how to do so. The "Stone Floor" contains five run of stones, producing two hundred and fifty barrels of flour per day—besides a proportionate quantity of the other articles manufactured at the mills. By processes of cleansing and preparing the wheat, cooling the flour, &c., &c., all as admirable, and on the same principle as those we have already alluded to, the Croton Mills make more flour from the same amount of wheat, than usual, and the flour itself is of a purer, better, and more uniform quality, and carried both premiums at the last Fair of the American Institute.

We have not yet said any thing of the manufacture of the *Farina* and *Wheaten Grits*—two articles of food which have already become extensively popular, being the most wholesome and nourishing forms in which the staff of life has ever been prepared. The Farina is the disembowelled kernel of the wheat, preserved in a granular form, and divested of every species of alloy and covering. Its preparation, we do not hesitate to say, is one of the most exquisitely beautiful processes to which machinery has ever been applied. At any rate, nothing at all to compare with it has ever come under our observation.

We have still left almost every thing unsaid, and yet our space is absolutely exhausted; and we must hasten to close our brief notice of the Croton Mills—strongly urging all who are interested in scientific discoveries, or love to watch the movements of Nature's forces controlled by human will, to pay the establishment a visit.

So much for a very imperfect description of a single establishment of New York. Now let us vacillate to a subject somewhat different, and which, had we the disposition, we might elongate into a volume by itself—even to *Gutta Percha*—of which we have learned the most interesting, the most incredible things, during a ramble through the extensive establishment of the *American Gutta Percha Company*, under the management of our enterprising fellow-citizen, S. T. Armstrong, Esq.

We have selected this subject, because it is one perhaps less generally known to our readers than any other, as the concluding illustration in our notice of the Manufactures of New York. It is doubtless true that Gutta Percha will, from its cheapness, its durability, and the facility with which it may be worked, vastly multiply the comforts of life, and bring within the reach of the man of taste, however limited his means, forms of elegance, and fac similes of the productions of genius, which he could not otherwise hope to possess. Already the American Gutta Percha Company has, under its exclusive patents, manufactured extensively, this article into Machine Belts and Bands, Gas and Water Pipes, Speaking Pipes, Insulators for Telegraph Wires, Saddles and Harness of all kinds, Trays, Fancy Boxes, Tables, Pumps, Boxes and Valves, Bookbinding, Vellum, Balls, Waterproof Roofing, Inkstands, Drinking-cups, Canes, Whips, Flasks, Hats, Caps, Boots and Shoes, Clothing, Decorations for Houses and Ship-cabins, Chairs, Lining for Bread-casks for sea-voyages, Air-tight Coffins, Linings for Water-tanks, Powder-kegs for the transportation of powder in water, Soda Fountains, Gasometers, Bottles, Picture and Looking-glass Frames, &c., &c. The demand for these manufactures far exceeds the present arrangements of the Company to supply: and we are happy to learn that the capital of the Company is to be increased, during the present year, from $50,000 to $150,000 or $200,000—and even this will be found probably insufficient. Indeed, nothing short of the establishment of manufactories in all parts of the country will ever be able at all to supply the demand. Besides the enumeration above, Gutta Percha has been found invaluable for many medical and surgical purposes, and in experimental organic chemistry—and a distinguished writer remarks, that were it only for its incalculable advantages when used in place of splints and bandages, in the case of fractures, it would be one of the greatest boons that discovery has ever conferred upon humanity. It has already been extensively approved for bougies, catheters, stethescopes, nipple-shells, bandages, &c., &c.; for preserving the strength of medicines of a volatile character, and in the application of galvanism and electricity to the healing art,—it being a perfect non-conductor. For marine and national purposes, the field is also most extensive; as inside sheathing for ships, for buoys and beacons, it is supposed to resist, for all time, vermin and decay. For army and navy equipments, canvas, deck-covers, car-covers, sails and rigging, it is admirable,—being impervious to damp, mildew and rot—as also for cannon-covers, water-tanks, *life-boats*, "Atkinson's" improved plan for relieving stranded and sunken vessels, for surf-boats, taking off cargoes, and lightening over sand-bars, and innumerable other applications, it is destined to supersede all other materials.

Gutta Percha was first introduced into England for manufacturing purposes, by Richard Archibald Brooman, to whom letters patent were granted in 1844 and 1845. Other patents were subsequently granted to other persons for its application to bookbinding, boots and shoes, hats, &c., &c.; and in 1846, letters patent were granted to a Quaker of Dublin, by name Bewley, for its application to the manufacture of flexible syringes, &c. Subsequently Bewley and others purchased all the patents in England, formed a gigantic company, enlisting in it many of the members of the East India Company, and at once commenced the manufacture of the article in all its then known branches—applying at the same time for patents in France, Germany and the United States. They also established agencies at Singapore, (East Indies,) and all along the Malay coast, (where alone the tree grows,) for the purpose of including in their monopoly the production of the raw material.

In the spring of 1847, our fellow-townsman, Mr. S. T. Armstrong, visited London, upon invitation, and perfected arrangements with the English company for the introduction of the Gutta Percha manufacture into the United States, and also for procuring the raw material. He returned in the fall; and having completed the necessary machinery, commenced the first manufacture of Gutta Percha in the United States. The business at once assumed an important rank, and has gone on steadily increasing; until, as has been already stated, the Company has found it absolutely necessary to triple or quadruple its present basis of operations.

Thus is our space twice over occupied, and we have mentioned but two out of our two thousand manufacturing establishments. We give up in despair.

www.ingramcontent.com/pod-product-compliance
Lightning Source LLC
LaVergne TN
LVHW021419110826
845150LV00007B/1997

9781425509163